# *365 Prayers*

Every day, a moment with Christ.

Anne-Marie Tremblay

Dear reader,

Welcome to 365 Prayers, an invitation to begin each day in communion with the voice of the divine, as expressed in the words of Christ. This book is a unique journey, an immersion in the love and wisdom of Jesus, where each prayer has been conceived as if Jesus himself were addressing it to us.

As the author of this collection, I felt the need to share a deeper, more personal experience of prayer. These prayers are not my own, but what I imagine to be the prayers of Jesus, expressed with unconditional love for each and every one of us. Through the universal themes of faith, love, forgiveness, gratitude and more, I hope you can connect more intimately with his presence.

"365 Prayers" is not just a book, it's an experience, a personal conversation with Jesus, one prayer a day for a whole year. It aims to accompany you through the different seasons of life, offering comfort in times of struggle, joy in times of happiness and wisdom in times of doubt.

I've tried to imagine what Jesus would say to our world today, how he would address our fears, our hopes, our struggles and our triumphs. It's my humble offering to help bridge the gap between everyday life and the spiritual life, to help make every day an opportunity to grow closer to

Jesus.

Finally, this book is an invitation. An invitation to let these prayers touch you, to make them your own, to use them as a starting point for your own dialogue with Jesus. Perhaps some days the words will resonate deeply with you, and other days they will challenge your perceptions. Whatever the case, I encourage you to welcome them with an open mind and a heart ready to be transformed.

I'm honoured to share this journey with you and hope that these prayers will bring you comfort, inspiration and a renewed sense of Jesus' presence in your life.

With gratitude and respect,

The author.

# January 1st

My dear child, welcome to this new year. Know that each day that dawns is a new opportunity for you to know My love and to draw closer to Me. Remember, "For I know the plans I have for you, says the Lord, plans for peace and not for evil, to give you a future and a hope" (Jeremiah 29:11). In times of joy, I share your happiness. In times of pain, I am there to comfort you. In times of doubt, I am there to enlighten you. As you begin this New Year, I ask you to keep your heart open to My presence. May you remember my love for you, every day of this New Year and always. May you find strength and comfort in My presence, and may you share that love with those around you. With love.

# 2 January

My dear child, on this second day of the year, remember My constant presence at your side. "Do not be afraid, for I am with you; do not be dismayed, for I am your God; I will strengthen you, I will help you, I will uphold you with my triumphant right hand" (Isaiah 41:10). In times of chaos, seek the silence where My voice is heard. I am the way, the truth and the life. When doubt and confusion arise, turn to Me. I am the light that illuminates your path, guiding you through every difficulty. Don't hesitate to confide in Me. I'm always ready to listen, to bring comfort and wisdom. May you find serenity in My presence today, knowing that I support you. With love.

# 3 January

On this new day, remember that I am your firm refuge, your steadfast support. The world may be tumultuous, but "The Lord is my shepherd; I shall not want" (Psalm 23:1). As you navigate through the uncertainty and challenges of the New Year, never forget that you are not going through these trials alone. I am at your side, giving you strength and courage, offering you the resilience to overcome all obstacles. Pray for health, for yourself and for those you love. I'm here to support your well-being, to heal and comfort you. Pray for your family, that I may protect and bless them with my inexhaustible love. Pray for your professional success, so that I can guide you and give you the wisdom you need to succeed. I am always by your side, even in the darkest moments. Every day, look for me and you will find me. In return, you'll find the peace, comfort and love that I'm always offering you. In gratitude and love.

# 4 January

Don't forget today that I'm with you always. Your health is a precious blessing, and I'm here to support and strengthen you in times of weakness. "He heals the brokenhearted and binds up their wounds" (Psalm 147:3). Look upon this New Year as an opportunity to focus on your well-being, and to take care of the precious gift of life I have given you. I'm here to help you feel strong, resilient and full of energy. In the same way, pray for the health of your loved ones. May my blessing envelop them, protect them, and give them the strength to overcome all difficulties. In all things, may you find peace in My presence and the assurance of My unconditional love for you. In trust and faith.

# 5 January

Today, I encourage you to reflect on your daily habits, those regular practices that shape your life. "Do not forsake your friend or your father's friend, and do not enter your brother's house in the day of your distress. Better is a neighbour near than a brother far off" (Proverbs 27:10). These words underline the importance of maintaining positive relationships. Take care of your health, nourish your body and mind with what is good, and cultivate compassion for others. Remember that I am always at your side, offering you my support and love. In gratitude and peace.

# 6 January - Epiphany

This Epiphany, remember the visit of the Magi to the infant Jesus, a moment of revelation and gratitude. "They came into the house, saw the child with Mary his mother, fell down and worshipped him; then they opened their treasures and gave him gifts of gold, frankincense and myrrh" (Matthew 2:11). May this day remind you of the importance of seeking the light in your life, honouring God's presence and sharing your gifts with others. As you celebrate Epiphany, know that I am with you, bringing you my peace and love. May your journey through this year lead you to moments of revelation and spiritual growth. Under heavenly guidance and love.

# 7 January

On this day, turn your gaze towards your professional aspirations and goals. "All work has its reward, but the words of the mouth lead only to scarcity" (Proverbs 14:23). Know that every effort you make is a step towards realising your dreams. When you encounter obstacles, remember that perseverance is the key to success. Ask me for wisdom and direction in your decisions, because I'm here to guide you and give you clarity. May you find satisfaction and fulfilment in your work, and may each day bring you closer to the success you deserve. With faith and perseverance.

# 8 January

On this day, I invite you to reflect on your mental and emotional health. "Do not be anxious about anything, but in everything by prayer and supplication with thanksgiving let your requests be made known to God" (Philippians 4:6). Worries and anxieties can sometimes overwhelm you, but remember that you are never alone in the face of these challenges. I'm here to bring you peace and comfort. Pray for inner peace and the strength to overcome emotional difficulties. Nourish your spirit with positive thoughts and an attitude of gratitude. May you find in Me the refuge and support you need to maintain your mental and emotional balance. In calm and trust.

## 9th January

On this day, I invite you to focus on the precious gift of life and the celebration of every moment. "I have set before you life and death, blessing and curse. Choose life, that you and your descendants may live" (Deuteronomy 30:19). Every day is a blessing, an opportunity to grow, to love and to live fully. Enjoy the simple moments, find joy in the little things and fill your heart with gratitude for every moment. I'm with you every step of the way, offering my love and guidance. May you embrace each day with joy and gratitude. In appreciation and celebration.

## 10 January

Today, think about the importance of faith in your life. "For we walk by faith, not by sight" (2 Corinthians 5:7). Faith is the compass that guides you through the storm, the anchor that holds you in place in times of uncertainty. Trust in my infinite love for you, even at times when you feel lost or afraid. Pray for the strength of your faith, for trust in my loving presence. May your faith give you the resilience you need to get through life's challenges and trials. Remember that I am always with you, guiding your steps with love. In faith and trust.

## January 11th

On this day, turn your thoughts to your family, that precious gift of love and support. "Honour thy father and thy mother, that thy days may be prolonged in the land which the Lord thy God giveth thee" (Exodus 20:12). Cherish the time you spend with them, for it is priceless. Know that you are a pillar for them, just as they are for you. Pray for their protection, well-being and happiness. Don't forget that I'm with you, guiding and supporting every member of your family. May you all feel my love and peace at every moment. In love and unity.

## 12 January

Today, I invite you to contemplate the wonderful gift of friendship. "He that hath many friends hath them to his hurt, but such a friend is dearer to him than a brother" (Proverbs 18:24). True friends are precious treasures, offering comfort, joy and support. Be grateful for these relationships and take the time to nurture them. Pray for your friends, for their well-being and happiness. May my blessings envelop them and may they know the assurance of my love. Remember that I am with you, guiding you in love and kindness. In friendship and brotherhood.

# 13 January

On this day, focus on the power of gratitude. "Give thanks in all things, for this is God's will for you in Christ Jesus" (1 Thessalonians 5:18). Gratitude can turn the simplest of days into a celebration of life. Take a moment to reflect on the blessings in your life, both large and small. Let your heart be filled with gratitude for these gifts, and let this gratitude become a source of joy and peace. I am with you every moment, offering you my love and grace. May you find joy in gratitude. In gratitude and celebration.

# 14 January

Today I invite you to think about kindness and compassion. "Be kind to one another, tenderhearted, forgiving one another, just as God in Christ forgave you" (Ephesians 4:32). Kindness and compassion are reflections of my love in you. When you show kindness to others, you are a beacon of light in the world. Pray for a heart filled with kindness, for the strength to show compassion, even in difficult times. Know that I am at your side, accompanying you with love in every act of kindness you perform. May you be an example of my goodness in the world. In kindness and compassion.

## 15 January

On this day, meditate on the virtue of patience. "But those who trust in the Lord renew their strength. They take flight, they soar like eagles; they run, and are not weary; they walk, and are not weary" (Isaiah 40:31). Patience is a strength that enables you to face uncertainty and challenges with serenity. Pray for the wisdom to understand that everything happens in its own time, for the patience to know how to wait for the perfect moment. Don't forget that I'm always with you, giving you my love and support in every moment of waiting. May you embrace patience as a gift, not a trial. In patience and faith.

## 16 January

Today, I invite you to focus on the beauty of the creation that surrounds you. "The heavens declare the glory of God, and the expanse proclaims the work of his hands" (Psalms 19:1). Every sunrise, every flower, every breath of fresh air is a reminder of my love for you. Pray for the preservation of this magnificent creation, for the wisdom to cherish and respect it. Know that I'm here to guide you, offering you my love and support in every moment of contemplation. May you find comfort and joy in the beauty of nature. In wonder and respect.

# 17 January

This day, turn to your inner potential. "I can do all things through him who strengthens me" (Philippians 4:13). You have an incredible reservoir of talent and ability within you. Pray for the strength and wisdom to tap into that potential, for the courage to take on new challenges and reach new heights. Know that I'm with you every step of the way, offering you my love and guidance. May you achieve everything you've imagined and even more. With strength and determination.

# 18th January

Today, I invite you to think about the importance of truth. "You will know the truth, and the truth will set you free" (John 8:32). Truth is a beacon, guiding your steps in the right direction and illuminating the dark areas of your life. Pray for the wisdom to always seek the truth, for the courage to speak it when necessary. Don't forget that I'm always with you, offering you my love and support in your quest for truth. May you always find the light in the truth. In your daily life, may truth be your ally, not only in your words but also in your actions. Every moment lived in truth is another step towards a life aligned with your values and convictions. Know that truth brings freedom, clarity and self-respect. Always seek the truth, even when it's hard to accept. Truth is your guide in the dark, a reliable compass on life's journey. In truth and in extended freedom.

# 19 January

Today, consider the value of perseverance. "Do not grow weary in doing good, for we will reap in due season, if we do not slacken" (Galatians 6:9). Perseverance is a quiet strength that keeps you going even when things are difficult. Pray for the strength to persevere, for the courage to keep going even when the going gets tough. Know that I am always with you, offering you my love and support, encouraging you in every step you take. May you always find the strength to persevere, knowing that every challenge you overcome brings you a little closer to your goals. In perseverance and courage.

# 20th January

This day, turn your attention to forgiveness. "If we confess our sins, he is faithful and just to forgive us our sins and to cleanse us from all unrighteousness" (1 John 1:9). Forgiveness has the power to heal wounded hearts and mend broken relationships. Pray for the courage to forgive those who have hurt you and for the grace to ask forgiveness when you have hurt others. Know that I am with you in these moments of forgiveness, bringing you my love and peace. May you find freedom and healing in forgiveness, and know that you are always loved, no matter what mistakes you may have made. In forgiveness and reconciliation.

## 21 January

On this day, think of the power of humility. "For everyone who exalts himself will be humbled, and he who humbles himself will be exalted" (Luke 14:11). Humility opens you to the understanding of others, allows you to learn and grow. Pray for a humble heart, for the wisdom to know when to listen, when to ask for help, and when to admit your mistakes. Know that I'm here, always ready to offer you my love and support in your moments of humility. May you find strength in humility and see its true value. In humility and learning.

## 22 January

Today, think about the concept of service. "For the Son of Man himself did not come to be served, but to serve, and to give his life as a ransom for many" (Mark 10:45). To serve others is to share my love with them. Pray that your heart will be ready to serve, that you will be willing to help and support those in need. Know that I am with you in every act of service, offering my love and my blessing. May you find pleasure in serving and giving, knowing that it is through these actions that you are truly blessed. In service and generosity.

## 23 January

Today, I invite you to meditate on peace. "I leave you peace, I give you my peace. I do not give to you as the world gives. Let not your heart be troubled, neither let it be alarmed" (John 14:27). Peace is not just the absence of conflict, it is a state of harmony and tranquillity that comes from within. Pray for peace in your heart, for serenity in your mind, even in the midst of the storm. Know that I am always with you, offering you my love and my peace. May you find peace in me, knowing that I am your refuge and your strength. In peace and tranquillity.

## 24 January

Today, think about gratitude. "Give thanks in all things, for this is God's will for you in Christ Jesus" (1 Thessalonians 5:18). Gratitude allows you to recognise and appreciate all the blessings in your life. Pray for a grateful heart, for the ability to see moments of joy and beauty even in difficult times. Know that I am always with you, offering you my love and gratitude for every step you take. May you find joy in gratitude and turn each day into a celebration of my blessings. In gratitude and thankfulness.

## 25 January

Today, focus on the importance of faith. "Faith is the assurance of things hoped for and the demonstration of things not seen" (Hebrews 11:1). Faith gives you assurance and hope in times of uncertainty. Pray for unshakeable faith, for the confidence to believe even when you can't see. Know that I am always with you, nourishing your faith, offering you my love and my presence. Seek to nourish your faith every day, through prayer, meditation on my word, and communion with others. May this faith give you the strength to overcome obstacles, the perseverance to stay on the path, and the confidence to know that you are loved and supported. May you walk by faith and not by sight, knowing that I guide your every step. In faith and hope.

## 26 January

On this day, meditate on charity. "Let not your charity be hypocritical. Abhor evil; hold fast to what is good" (Romans 12:9). Charity goes beyond material help; it is an act of selfless love towards others. Pray for a charitable heart, for the desire to help and to give without expecting anything in return. Know that I am with you in every act of charity, offering you my love and my blessing. May your charity be a light in the darkness for those who need it, and a testimony of my love for all. In charity and love.

## 27 January

Today, consider the importance of patience. "But if we hope for what we do not see, we wait for it with patience" (Romans 8:25). Patience helps you to wait in faith and trust, knowing that everything happens in its own time. Pray for a patient heart, for the ability to wait without getting discouraged, knowing that each moment has its own purpose. Know that I am always with you in your moments of waiting, offering you my love and my peace. May you always be patient, knowing that I am at work even when you can't see it. In patience and trust.

## 28 January

Today, think about the value of integrity. "He who walks in integrity walks in confidence, But he who takes crooked ways will be found out" (Proverbs 10:9). Integrity invites you to be true, honest and just in all your actions and decisions. Pray for a spirit of integrity, for the strength to do what is right even when it is difficult. Know that I am with you in every choice you make, offering my love and support. May you live with integrity, faithfully reflecting my teachings, and inspire others by your example. In integrity and truth.

## 29 January

On this day, reflect on the value of kindness towards others. "Let all bitterness, animosity, wrath, clamour, slander, and malice depart from your heart" (Ephesians 4:31). Pay attention to your heart and cultivate kindness and compassion towards your fellow human beings. Be ready to reach out and offer support without judgement or expectation. Let your behaviour reflect God's love and goodness, promoting peace and harmony in your interactions. May each of your acts of kindness bring a ray of light and comfort to those in need. In kindness and true love.

## 30th January

On this day, I invite you to meditate on the value of patience and to place your trust in me. "I am with you always, to the end of the age" (Matthew 28:20). Become aware of the importance of patience in your life and ask for my help to develop this virtue. Let your heart be filled with confidence, knowing that I am the faithful God who guides your steps and works in all things for your good. May you find inner peace and serenity in knowing that I am at your side, offering you my love and guidance at every moment. With patience and trust in me.

## 31 January

On this last day of the month, I invite you to reflect on the value of perseverance. "Let perseverance do its work perfectly, so that you may be perfect and complete, failing in nothing" (James 1:4). Life is full of challenges and obstacles, but perseverance enables you to overcome these difficulties and keep moving forward. Pray for the inner strength and determination not to give up in the face of adversity. Know that every step of your journey is an opportunity to grow and learn. May your perseverance be nourished by hope and faith in a better future. I'm always here, encouraging you and supporting you in your efforts. May you find the strength and courage to persevere, knowing that your efforts are precious and that they will lead you to the fulfilment of your deepest aspirations. With perseverance and confidence.

## February 1st

On this first day of the month, I invite you to meditate on the value of trusting in me. "Trust in the Lord with all your heart, and lean not on your own wisdom" (Proverbs 3:5). Trust in me allows you to let go of your own concerns and place your path in my hands. Pray for the ability to trust in me fully, knowing that I am always there to love, guide and protect you. May you find peace and security in knowing that you don't have to control everything, but can rely on my wisdom and guidance. In trust and surrender.

## 2 February

On this second day of the month, I invite you to meditate on the value of being kind to yourself. "Love your neighbour as yourself" (Mark 12:31). Remember how precious you are and how unconditionally loved by me. Allow my love to fill your heart and guide you in how you see yourself. Pray that you will treat yourself with kindness, forgive yourself for past mistakes and give yourself a new chance every day. You deserve to be loved and respected, including by yourself. Allow yourself time to take care of your physical, emotional and spiritual well-being. May you cultivate healthy self-esteem and unlimited compassion for yourself. I am at your side, supporting and encouraging you to embrace kindness towards yourself in every aspect of your life. In my unconditional love and kindness to you.

## 3 February

Today, I invite you to meditate on the value of gratitude. "Give thanks in all things, for this is God's will for you in Christ Jesus" (1 Thessalonians 5:18). I remind you of the importance of cultivating an attitude of gratitude in your life. Take a moment to reflect on the countless blessings that surround you, large and small. Let your heart be filled with gratitude for the blessings you have received. Pray that this gratitude will inspire you to live each day with joy and to share this gratitude with those around you. Know that I am at your side, supporting you and encouraging you to maintain an attitude of gratitude in all aspects of your life. May your gratitude light up your life and bring an abundance of peace and happiness. In love and infinite gratitude.

# 4 February

Today I remind you of the importance of encouraging one another. Remember my words: "Rejoice with those who rejoice; weep with those who weep" (Romans 12:15). Be a source of comfort and support to your brothers and sisters. Share their joys and sorrows, and show my love through your words and actions. Pray that I will guide you in your role of encouragement, bringing unconditional support and hope to the lives of others. Together, in mutual encouragement and love, let us grow in faith and be an inspiration to those around us.

# 5 February :

On this blessed day, I invite you to come closer to me, Jesus. Seek my presence in every moment and let my peace flood your heart. Be a channel of love and compassion to those around you, spreading my light into their lives. Nourish your soul with my word and meditate on my teachings, for they will guide you on the path to truth and fulfilment. Take care of yourself physically, emotionally and spiritually, for you are precious to me. Entrust your concerns to me and let me support you in your trials. Remember that I'm always here, with you every step of the way. May your day be blessed by my loving presence, and may you feel my peace that passes all understanding.

# 6 February

On this blessed day, I invite you to cultivate gratitude in your life. Take time to acknowledge the many blessings you have received. Express your gratitude to me, Jesus, for all the graces that have been showered upon you. Let your gratitude be shown not only in words, but also in deeds. Share your love and generosity with those in need, show compassion for others and bring a touch of light and hope into their lives. Remember that gratitude opens the door to joy and inner peace. Pray that I will help you to cultivate a grateful heart every day, so that you can live in the fullness of my blessings. May your day be filled with gratitude and thankfulness to me, your Lord and Saviour.

# 7 February

Today I invite you to pay special attention to your health. Pray for your physical, mental and emotional well-being, entrusting your concerns to me and asking me for the strength and healing you need. Realise the value of your body and mind, and thank me for the gifts of health and vitality. Take concrete steps to look after yourself, by adopting a balanced lifestyle, exercising regularly and nourishing your body with healthy foods. Entrust your health into my loving hands, and know that I am always present to bring you healing, comfort and restoration. May this day be an opportunity to take care of yourself and cultivate flourishing health in all aspects of your life.

# 8 February

Cultivate love and respect for your family. Appreciate each member and support them with all your heart. Be attentive to their needs, listen to them with compassion and open-mindedness. Be patient and understanding of their differences. Pray for unity and harmony in your family, so that the ties that bind you grow stronger every day. May peace and love fill every moment spent together. I'm here to guide and accompany you on the path of family life.

# 9 February

On this day, I invite you to cultivate love and kindness in your relationships with others. Be patient, a good listener and understanding. Express your gratitude for the positive connections in your life. Let your interactions be marked by love and respect. I'm here to support you in this process.

My child, I guide you in your quest for harmonious relationships. Let my love flow through you, illuminating the hearts of those around you. Let your presence reflect my light and bear witness to my infinite love.

Amen.

# 10 February

Open your heart to love and compassion on this day. Be attentive to the needs of others and offer them your support. Pray for patience and acceptance in your relationships. Meditate on my word for strength and inspiration. Let your presence radiate love and peace. I am with you, guiding your steps towards harmony and serenity. May every encounter be an opportunity to spread love and joy. May your actions be marked by kindness and generosity. May every word you speak be a source of comfort and encouragement. May your life be a living testimony to my infinite love.

# 11 February

On this day dedicated to work, I send you my blessing. Pray for wisdom and perseverance in your professional activities. May your work reflect your faith in God and be a testimony to your commitment. Be attentive to the needs of your colleagues and cultivate relationships based on respect and mutual support. Entrust your concerns to me and find peace and guidance in me. Go forward with determination, knowing that I'm with you every step of the way.

# 12 February

My child, on this day, my advice to you is patience and endurance. Every trial is an opportunity for growth, embrace it with courage. Look for the good in every situation, there is always a lesson to be learned. Remember, you have immense strength within you. May you use it to overcome obstacles. Remember to love unconditionally, as the Father loves you. Take care of your neighbour, for we are all brothers and sisters. Be a light and a hope in this world.

# 13 February

Dear child, today is a new dawn. Greet it with gratitude and hope. Every breath, every moment is a precious gift. Consider the small pleasures, the simple moments. They are the fabric of your existence. Don't forget to appreciate the people around you, and the beauties of nature that delight you.

Cultivate compassion for yourself and others. It's a balm for the soul and builds bridges of love and understanding. Share, because in giving we receive. The happiness found in sharing is an incomparable joy.

Forgive sincerely. Forgiveness is a liberation, a flight to peace and tranquillity. It erases the chains of the past and gives you a new freedom. May your heart be light and your mind serene. We pray Amen.

# 14 February

My child, on this special day I remind you of one of my best-known parables - that of the Good Samaritan (Luke 10:25-37). On this day, may you remember that the true measure of love lies not in grand gestures, but in the daily compassion you show to those around you, even the most despised or neglected.

Like the Samaritan who helped the wounded stranger by the roadside, may you always be ready to reach out and help those in need. May you understand that love and compassion know no borders, judge nothing and ask nothing in return.

Love is patient, love is helpful, love is not envious. Love does not boast or puff itself up (1 Corinthians 13:4). On this day of love, may you love as I have loved, with an open and generous heart. Amen.

# 15 February

Precious child, today I remind you of the words I spoke in the Sermon on the Mount: "Blessed are the pure in heart, for they shall see God" (Matthew 5:8). May this truth guide you this day. May you keep your heart pure and sincere, not only towards others, but also towards yourself.

Honour the truth in all things, for it is the light that dispels the shadows of deception. May you walk with integrity and uprightness, even if the path seems difficult. May you be a force for truth and goodness in a world that desperately needs it.

## 16 February

Dear child, I invite you today to remember these words: "Ask, and it will be given to you; seek, and you will find; knock, and it will be opened to you" (Matthew 7:7). Don't hesitate to seek, to ask questions, to explore. Truth reveals itself to those who seek it with a sincere heart.

Learn to let go and entrust your worries to the Father. He is in control, even when everything seems chaotic. May you find peace in His presence, and the courage to carry on despite the difficulties.

Remember that you are loved, that you are precious, that you have a purpose. Every day is a new opportunity to grow, to love, to make a difference. May you welcome each new day with an open heart and a ready mind. Amen.

## 17 February

Today, my child, I direct you to the story of David and Goliath (1 Samuel 17). Remember how David, armed only with his faith and a slingshot, was able to defeat the fearsome giant. Let this story remind you that, no matter how great your challenges, they are no greater than your faith.

Never forget that you are never alone in your struggles. The Father is always with you, giving you the strength and courage you need to overcome every trial. Do not fear failure, for even in failure there is a valuable lesson to be learned.

Trust in Him, persevere in your faith and your efforts. May you find the courage to face your own Goliaths, armed with your faith and your hope. Amen.

## 18 February

My child, today I remind you of the words I spoke: "Love your enemies, do good to those who hate you" (Luke 6:27). May you remember that true love makes no distinction and seeks no revenge.

In the face of hostility, choose compassion. In the face of contempt, choose understanding. For hatred only fans the flames of hatred, but love has the power to extinguish its flames.

Where you find offence, may you forgive. Where you find discord, may you be a peacemaker. Remember, every act of love transforms the world, one heart at a time. Amen.

## 19 February

Today I invite you to remember the parable of the sower (Matthew 13:1-23). Like seeds that fall on different soils, the Word of God can be received in different ways. May you be like the good soil that receives the Word, understands it and bears fruit.

Take the time to nourish your mind and soul with the Word of God. Meditate on it, understand it and let it light your way. May you be a living example of God's love, a light in a world that needs hope.

Where you see fear, sow love. Where you see discord, sow peace. Every day is an opportunity to sow seeds of kindness and compassion. May you make your life a fertile field for God's love. Amen.

## 20 February

My child, I encourage you today to remember the parable of the prodigal son (Luke 15:11-32). This story illustrates the Father's unreserved forgiveness, no matter how far we stray. Never be afraid to come back to Him, no matter how lost you feel.

May you embrace mercy and forgiveness in your own life. Forgive yourself for past mistakes and forgive those who have hurt you. Forgiveness frees your heart from bitterness and opens the way to healing and peace.

Remember that you are always loved, always welcomed by the Father. No error is too great, no fault too serious to escape His unconditional love. May you find comfort and strength in this truth. Amen.

## 21 February

My dear child, on this day, remember Paul's words to the Ephesians: "Do not be overcome by evil, but overcome evil with good" (Romans 12:21). In a world where evil sometimes seems to triumph, may you be a force for good, a living example of God's goodness.

Every act of kindness, however small, is a ray of light in the darkness. May you always choose to be kind, even when it's difficult. May you find in yourself the courage to stand up for what is right, to show compassion for the oppressed and to bear witness to the Father's love. Goodness has the power to transform the world, one gesture at a time. Don't underestimate the impact you can have. Do good, not because others deserve it, but because it's what you're called to do. Amen.

## 22 February

My child, today I remind you of my promise: "I am with you always, to the end of the age" (Matthew 28:20). Never forget that you are never alone, even in your darkest hour.

May you feel my presence in you, around you, in every moment of joy, in every challenge. Don't be afraid of loneliness, because I'm here. Don't be afraid of failure, because I'm here to help you get back on your feet.

On this day, may my presence give you the courage to face your fears, pursue your dreams and live your life with love and compassion. Know that you are loved, today and always. Amen.

## 23 February

Today I invite you to meditate on the story of Job, a man who suffered immense tribulations, but who never lost faith in God. May you find in this story the strength to remain faithful, even in times of trial and doubt.

When you're going through a storm, remember that the sun always shines above the clouds. The trial is temporary, but God's love is eternal. Don't let grief cloud your faith or make you forget the many blessings in your life.

Every day is a new opportunity to draw closer to God, to deepen your faith and your resilience. May you find refuge and indomitable strength in Him. Amen.

## 24 February

Today, I encourage you to remember the story of the healing of the blind man in Bethsaida (Mark 8:22-26). Remember how, even after being touched by me the first time, the man's vision was still blurred, and I had to touch him a second time to fully restore his sight.

Sometimes healing, change and growth take time. Don't give up if you don't see results straight away. May you have the patience and faith to persevere, to keep searching, hoping and praying, even when the answer seems slow in coming.

Always remember that the Father works according to His own timetable, not ours. Trust in Him and know that whatever happens, happens in its own time. Amen.

## 25 February

Today, my child, let yourself be inspired by the parable of the talents (Matthew 25:14-30). Each person receives unique gifts from God. May you use your talents, not for your own glory, but for the good of others and for the glory of God.

Don't hide your talents for fear of failure or judgement. Let them shine, for they are a gift from God to be shared with the world. May you be bold in using your gifts to make a positive difference in the lives of others.

Always remember that the true value of a talent lies in its use, not in its possession. May you find joy and meaning in using your gifts to serve and love others. Amen.

## 26 February

Today I invite you to meditate on the words of the apostle Paul: "Do not be conformed to this world, but be transformed by the renewal of your mind" (Romans 12:2). The world can often push us towards selfishness, competition and materialism, but you are called to a higher life.

May you resist the lure of the world and seek to do God's will. Seek truth, justice, love and peace. May you find the courage to make decisions that are in line with your faith, even if they are unpopular.

Every day, renew your mind through prayer, meditation and study of the Word of God. May you be transformed from within and be a shining light in this world. Amen.


## 27 February

My child, today remember the woman at the well (John 4:1-26). Despite her many mistakes and the judgement of society, I welcomed her with love and compassion. That's how God sees you: not as the world sees you, but through the prism of His unconditional love.

No matter what your past mistakes, no matter how many others may judge you, know that you are precious and loved in God's eyes. He alone knows the true value of your heart, and His love for you is unshakeable.

On this day, may you see yourself through God's eyes: a precious being, worthy of love and respect. Never let the opinions of others define your worth. You are loved, today and always. Amen.

# 28 February

On this day, I remind you of the words of the psalmist: "Yea, though I walk through the valley of the shadow of death, I will fear no evil, for thou art with me" (Psalm 23:4). Let this serve as a reminder that even in the darkest of times, you are never alone. Life can be full of challenges and difficulties, but don't be discouraged. May you find in me the strength to persevere, to keep hope even in the face of adversity. I'm with you every step of the way, supporting you, guiding you, loving you.

Always remember that God's presence is stronger than any fear, pain or doubt. With Him by your side, you can face any challenge. May you find comfort and courage in this truth. Amen.

# 29 February

Today is a rare day, just as each of you is unique and precious in God's eyes. Just as I fed the multitude with five loaves and two fish (Matthew 14:13-21), may you realise that even what seems small and insignificant can be used by God in extraordinary ways.

Don't underestimate your value or your potential. Every gesture of love, every act of kindness, every word of encouragement you offer can have an immense impact. May you be an instrument of God's goodness in the world, a reflection of His love and mercy.

On this rare day, may you recognise the rarity and value of each moment you are given to live. Each day is a gift. May you live fully, love freely and serve joyfully. Amen.

# 1st March

On this first day of the month, I invite you to reflect on the parable of the mustard seed (Matthew 13:31-32). The smallest of seeds can become the largest of trees. That's how the kingdom of heaven is, and that's how your faith can be.

Even if your faith seems small today, know that it has the potential to grow beyond what you can imagine. May you nourish it every day through prayer, meditation and acts of love and compassion.

Don't be discouraged if the changes you want to see in your life don't happen immediately. Just as a seed needs time to grow, your faith and your spiritual transformation need time to develop. May you have the patience and perseverance to keep believing, even when you can't see the results. Amen.

# 2 March

Today, my child, reflect on the teaching of the Sermon on the Mount (Matthew 5-7). I particularly encourage you to meditate on the notion of "blessed are the meek, for they shall inherit the earth" (Matthew 5:5). Gentleness is often misunderstood in today's world. It is perceived as a weakness, but in truth it is a strength. To be gentle is to choose to respond with love and patience, even in the face of provocation.

May you strive to embody gentleness in your interactions with others. Resist the urge to react with anger or hostility. Instead, choose love, patience and understanding. May you be a source of peace and kindness in this world. Amen.

# 3 March

Today, I invite you to meditate on the story of Zacchaeus (Luke 19:1-10). Even though he was a hated tax collector, Zacchaeus sought me out, and I accepted his invitation to share a meal. In response, Zacchaeus turned his life around, promising to repay those he had cheated.

This story shows that no one is beyond the reach of God's grace. Whatever your past mistakes, God is always ready to receive you with love and give you a new chance.

On this day, may you remember that you are worthy of God's love and grace. May you find the courage to turn to Him, to ask forgiveness and to make the changes necessary to live a more loving and just life. Amen.

# 4 March

Today, I remind you of the words of Paul in his letter to the Galatians: "Let us not grow weary in doing good, for we will reap in due season, if we do not grow weary" (Galatians 6:9). In a world often focused on immediacy, patience can be a difficult virtue to cultivate.

However, I encourage you to persevere in your efforts to do good, even if you don't immediately see the fruits of your labour. The good you sow today may bear unexpected and magnificent fruit in the future.

On this day, may you feel encouraged to continue doing good. Don't let the apparent silence discourage you, or tire of doing what is right. Your reward will come in time. Amen.

# 5 March

Today, I invite you to meditate on the story of Jonah. Even after fleeing from God and ending up in the belly of a great fish, Jonah was forgiven and used by God to deliver a message of repentance to Nineveh.

Remember that no matter how lost or distant you feel from God, He is always ready to forgive you and bring you back. There is grace and forgiveness in abundance for those who sincerely seek His face.

Don't let shame or regret keep you from God's love. No matter what you do wrong, you always have a place with Him. On this day, may you open your heart to His grace and forgiveness. May you find peace and restoration in Him. Amen.

# 6 March

Today, meditate on the story of the Good Samaritan (Luke 10:25-37). In this parable, it was the Samaritan, a foreigner, who showed true compassion towards the injured man, while others who should have helped passed by.

This story encourages you to show love and compassion to everyone, regardless of their background, beliefs or circumstances. May you strive to be a Good Samaritan in your own world, taking the time to help those in need.

On this day, may you be aware of the people around you who may need your help or compassion. May you be a source of kindness and mercy in their lives. Amen.

# 7 March

Today, reflect on my words in the book of John: "I am the light of the world. Whoever follows me will not walk in darkness, but will have the light of life" (John 8:12). In a world that can sometimes seem dark and confusing, I offer you a light to guide your steps.

May you seek this light in your life, finding it in prayer, meditation and reading the Scriptures. May you be guided by it in your decisions and actions. May you also be a light to others, reflecting God's love, goodness and truth to the world.

Always remember that even in the deepest darkness, God's light is never extinguished. May you find comfort, hope and courage in this truth. Amen.


# 8 March


Today, remember the story of Mary Magdalene (John 20:1-18). She was the first to see me risen and to tell the other disciples the good news. In her, we see an example of profound faith and devotion.

May you follow the example of Mary Magdalene in your own life. Seek me with perseverance, even in times of doubt and despair. Be ready to share the hope and love you find in me with others.

On this day, may you feel called to be a witness to the Resurrection in the world. May you share the good news of God's love and mercy with everyone you meet. Amen.

# 9 March

On this day, I remind you of the words in the book of Genesis: "God saw everything that he had made, and behold, it was very good" (Genesis 1:31). In every one of God's creations there is an inherent beauty and goodness.

May you see the beauty and goodness in and around you today. May it remind you how precious you are in God's eyes, and how much of a gift the world you live in is. May you celebrate and preserve this goodness by respecting life and God's creation.

On this day, may you commit yourself to seeing the good and the beautiful in all things, and to being an agent of goodness and beauty in the world. Amen.


# 10 March

Today, I invite you to meditate on the passage from the Gospel according to Matthew: "Come to me, all you who are weary and heavy laden, and I will give you rest" (Matthew 11:28). In me you can find the rest and peace you seek.

If you feel exhausted by life's challenges, know that you can always come to me. I'm here to carry your burdens with you. May you find in me the relief of your worries and the renewal of your spirit.

On this day, may you find rest in me. May you remember that you are never alone in your trials. I am with you, supporting you always. Amen.

## 11 March

Today I encourage you to meditate on the story of the woman at the well (John 4:1-26). This woman, despite her past mistakes and sins, was welcomed by me with love and compassion. I offered this woman of Samaria the water of eternal life, a sign of God's infinite grace.

No matter what your past, your mistakes or your regrets, know that you are always worthy of God's love. You are precious in His eyes and He wants you just as you are.

On this day, may you remember that you are deeply loved by God. May you open yourself to His love and grace, and let this knowledge transform you from within. May you share that love with everyone you meet. Amen.

## 12 March

Today, meditate on the story of the prodigal son (Luke 15:11-32). Even after squandering his inheritance and falling to his lowest depths, the son returned to his father, who welcomed him with love and joy. This parable illustrates God's inexhaustible mercy.

No matter how lost or distant you may feel from God, He is always waiting for you with open arms. He welcomes you back and is ready to forgive you.

On this day, may you turn to God with an open and repentant heart. May you experience His unconditional love and endless mercy. May you remember that you are always welcome in God's house. Amen.

# 13 March

Today, remember my words in the book of Matthew: "Where your treasure is, there will your heart be also" (Matthew 6:21). The things you value largely determine the direction of your life.

I invite you to think about what you really value. Is it wealth, power, personal success? Or is it love, compassion and service to others? May you choose to value what is truly eternal.

On this day, may you seek to align your heart with the treasures of God's kingdom. May you find your greatest joy and satisfaction in love, justice and mercy. Amen.

# 14 March

Today, think about these words from Revelation: "Behold, I stand at the door and knock. If anyone hears my voice and opens the door, I will come in to him and dine with him, and he with me" (Revelation 3:20). I'm always ready to come into your life, if you open the door of your heart to me.

Don't let fear, doubt or indifference keep you from me. May you have the courage to open your heart to my presence and my love.

On this day, may you feel my presence in your life. May you respond to my call with a heart that is open and ready to receive me. May you know the joy and peace that come from communion with me. Amen.

# 15 March

Today, I invite you to meditate on the story of the man born blind (John 9:1-41). Although he was born blind, this man received his sight through my power. It is a reminder that, whatever our difficulties or limitations, God can work miracles in our lives.

Don't despair when faced with obstacles that seem insurmountable. With God, nothing is impossible. He has the power to transform even the most difficult situations for our good.

Today, may you trust in God's power. May you bring your challenges and difficulties to Him, with the faith that He can transform them. May you be open to God's miracles in your life. Amen.


# 16 March

Today I encourage you to meditate on the story of the multiplication of the loaves (Mark 6:30-44). In this story, with just five loaves and two fish, I fed a crowd of five thousand people. This shows that God can take our limited resources and multiply them to accomplish great things.

Don't be discouraged if you feel inadequate or limited. God can use what you have to accomplish His purposes. Give Him what you have, no matter how small it may seem, and watch Him work wonders.

On this day, may you have faith in God's ability to use what you have to bless others. May you be willing to give generously, knowing that God is a multiplying God. Amen.

# 17 March

Today, consider these words from Luke's Gospel: "Love your enemies, do good to those who hate you" (Luke 6:27). This is one of the most difficult commandments, but also one of the most transforming.

This does not mean that you should approve or ignore the harmful actions of others, but rather that you should refuse to let yourself be carried away by hatred or resentment. May you find the strength to respond to hatred with love and to injustice with compassion.

Today, I ask you to pray for those who have hurt you. May you find the strength to love as God loves, unconditionally and without prejudice. Amen.


# 18th March

Today, I invite you to meditate on these words from the book of Proverbs: "The tongue has the power of life and death; those who love it will eat of its fruit" (Proverbs 18:21). The words you use have great power - they can hurt or heal, destroy or build.

May you be aware of the power of your words and choose to use that power for good. Speak with kindness and respect. Encourage those who are down. Praise goodness when you see it.

On this day, I ask you to make a conscious effort to use your words to bless others. May you recognise the power you hold and use it wisely. Amen.

# 19 March

Today, remember the story of the calmed storm (Mark 4:35-41). Even in the midst of the storm, when my disciples were terrified, I calmed the waters. This reminds you that, even in the midst of the storms of life, I am with you.

Don't let fear overwhelm you. Trust me, even when the circumstances seem hopeless. May you find peace in my presence, knowing that I can calm the most violent storm.

On this day, I ask you to trust me, even in the midst of the storms of your life. May you find peace in my presence and the courage to keep moving forward. Amen.

# 20 March

Today I remind you of my words in John's Gospel: "I am the good shepherd. The good shepherd lays down his life for his sheep" (John 10:11). I am your guide, ready to lead you through the green pastures and dark valleys of life.

Trust me to guide you. May you follow my paths and listen to my voice. Even if the path seems uncertain, I'm with you and I'll guide you.

On this day, may you have the faith to follow where I lead you. May you remember that I am the good shepherd, always ready to lead you to greener pastures. Amen.

# 21 March

Today I remind you of the parable of the sower (Matthew 13:1-23). The teaching here is to become like good soil, which receives God's word, understands it and produces an abundant harvest.

I invite you to open your heart to the Word of God. Let it take root in your life and produce good fruit. Don't let the worries of the world or the seduction of riches stifle the word.

On this day, may you be like the good earth, ready to receive God's word and let it transform your life. May you produce an abundant harvest of justice, peace and love. Amen.

# 22 March

Today, think about the story of the unforgiving servant (Matthew 18:21-35). This man received great mercy from his master, but refused to show the same mercy to another servant who owed him much less. For this, he was severely reprimanded.

This parable teaches us the importance of forgiveness. As we have been forgiven by God, we must also forgive others.

Today, I ask you to release any resentment or bitterness you may be holding inside. May you find the strength to forgive as you have been forgiven. May you live in the freedom and peace that come from forgiveness. Amen.

## 23 March

Today, think of the story of the woman who touched the edge of my cloak (Mark 5:25-34). Even in the crowd, her act of faith did not go unnoticed. She was healed, not because of her touch, but because of her faith.

God sees your faith, no matter how small or insignificant it may seem to you. May you have the confidence to turn to Him, even in the most desperate times.

On this day, I encourage you to draw close to God with bold faith. Know that He sees you, that He cares for you, and that He is able to heal and restore. Amen.

## 24 March

Today, meditate on the story of the persistent widow (Luke 18:1-8). This widow never stopped asking for justice, despite the judge's indifference. Her perseverance finally bore fruit.

This parable reminds us of the importance of perseverance in prayer. Even if you don't immediately see the answers to your prayers, don't give up. God hears every prayer and answers in His perfect time.

On this day, may you be persevering in prayer, knowing that God is faithful to answer. Even in the face of challenges, do not lose hope, but continue to pray with faith. Amen.

## 25 March

Today, reflect on the story of the barren fig tree (Luke 13:6-9). After several years without bearing fruit, the vinedresser decided to give it another chance and to give it special care.

This parable reminds us that God is patient with us, always giving us the opportunity to improve and bear fruit. He never tires of giving us another chance.

On this day, I encourage you to use the opportunities God has given you to do good and to grow spiritually. Don't give in to discouragement, but take courage and move forward with faith and hope. Amen.


## 26 March

Today, consider the story of the multiplication of the loaves and fishes (John 6:1-15). A little boy offers what he has, even if it seems insignificant compared to the need. And yet, with this small offering, I am feeding a multitude.

This miracle shows you that what you have to offer, however small it may seem to you, can be put to extraordinary use when you give it in faith.

On this day, may you give generously of what you have, of your time, your talents, your love. May you remember that every gesture of love and generosity counts, no matter how small. Amen.

# 27 March

Consider today the story of Martha and Mary (Luke 10:38-42). Martha was absorbed in service, while Mary chose to sit at my feet and listen to my word. I encouraged Martha to choose what was most important, as Mary did.

This doesn't mean that the service is bad, but rather that taking the time to stay in my presence and listen to my word is essential.

Today, may you take time to sit in silence, to read the Word of God and to pray. May you find a balance between service and rest, between action and contemplation. Amen.

# 28 March

Today, think about the story of the rich fool (Luke 12:16-21). This man accumulated wealth for himself, but was not rich towards God. He did not understand that life does not consist of an abundance of possessions.

This parable invites you to consider where your treasures lie. Don't let yourself be seduced by the pursuit of material riches, but seek to be rich towards God.

On this day, may you remember that the real treasure is in God. May you live not to accumulate material goods, but to love God and your neighbour. Amen.

# 29th March

Today, think about the story of the lost sheep (Luke 15:1-7). Even though only one sheep is lost among many, the shepherd leaves the ninety-nine to find it, showing the importance of each individual.

This parable reminds you that you are precious in God's eyes. He looks for you when you are lost and rejoices when you return to Him.

On this day, I remind you that you are invaluable to God. Wherever you are, you are loved and precious in His eyes. May you feel loved and welcomed in His presence. Amen.

# 30th March

Today, meditate on the story of the workers of the eleventh hour (Matthew 20:1-16). Despite their late arrival, they received the same wages as those who had worked all day. This shows God's generosity and His grace, which is given to everyone, no matter when they come to Him.

This parable reminds us that God is just, but His justice is not like that of the world. He is generous and gives more than we deserve.

On this day, may you remember that God is generous and loving. May you turn to Him with confidence, knowing that He will welcome you with love and grace, no matter when you come to Him. Amen.

# 31 March

Today, think about the story of the mustard seed (Matthew 13:31-32). Although it is the smallest of seeds, once planted it grows into a large tree.

This parable illustrates how the kingdom of God can start with seemingly insignificant things and end up growing and transforming everything around it.

On this day, I remind you that even the smallest gestures of love and acts of faith can have a great impact. May you sow seeds of kindness and love, hoping and believing that they will grow and bear fruit. Amen.

# 1st April

Today, meditate on the story of the ten virgins (Matthew 25:1-13). Five of them were prepared and had brought enough oil for their lamps, while the others were not ready for the bridegroom's return.

This parable reminds us of the importance of being spiritually prepared, of living each day as if it were the day of my return.

On this day, I encourage you to live in expectation of my return, not with fear, but with joy and preparation. May you seek to grow in your faith every day, so that you are ready at any moment. Amen.

## 2 April

Today, remember the story of Zacchaeus (Luke 19:1-10). Zacchaeus was a hated tax collector, but I chose to eat at his table. His encounter with me transformed his life and he chose to pay back those he had deceived.

This story shows that no one is beyond my grace and love. Everyone has the potential to be transformed by an encounter with me.

Today, may you be open to God's transforming work in your life. May you also see others not for what they are now, but for what they can become in Christ. Amen.

## 3 April

Meditate today on the story of the calmed storm (Mark 4:35-41). My disciples, frightened by the storm, woke me up. I calmed it and asked them why they were so afraid, where their faith lay.

This story reminds you that even in the midst of life's storms, I am with you. Don't let fear overwhelm you, but trust in me, for I have the power to calm the storms.

On this day, may you find peace in me, despite the storms you may go through. May you remember that I am always with you, ready to give you peace. Amen.

# 4 April

Today, I invite you to think about the story of the woman who lost her blood (Mark 5:25-34). Despite twelve years of suffering and isolation, she had faith that if she just touched my clothes, she would be healed. And that's exactly what happened.

This story shows the importance of faith and the impact it can have on our lives. No matter how hopeless a situation seems, there is always hope in me.

On this day, may you come to me in faith, even in difficult times. May you remember that I am your hope and your refuge. Amen.

# 5 April

Today, let's reflect on the story of the lost coin (Luke 15:8-10). A woman loses one of her ten coins and sweeps her house until she finds it. She is overjoyed when she finds it.

This parable underlines the value God places on each person and the joy he feels when a lost person is found.

On this day, remember that you are precious in God's eyes. He seeks you constantly and rejoices when you turn to Him. Amen.

# 6 April

Today, meditate on the story of the tower of Siloam (Luke 13:1-5). I warned that those who perished when the tower fell were no more guilty than others. I used this event to call everyone to repentance.

This story reminds us that tragedies are not always the result of individual sin, and that it is important to focus on our own repentance and spiritual growth.

On this day, may you concentrate on your own spiritual journey, always seeking to grow and draw closer to God. Amen.

# 7 April

Today, think about the story of the healing of the man born blind (John 9:1-7). I healed a man who was born blind, not because of his sin or that of his parents, but so that the works of God might be made manifest in him.

This story reminds us that God can use any situation, even those that seem tragic, to show His glory and His love.

On this day, may you remember that God can turn all situations for good. May you trust in Him in all your circumstances, knowing that He works for good. Amen.

# 8 April

Today, let's reflect instead on the story of the healing of the paralytic at Bethesda (John 5:1-9). This man waited 38 years to be healed. When I asked him if he wanted to be healed, he expressed despair because he had no one to help him. But I acted with compassion and healed him.

This story reminds us that I am always present, even in our darkest and most desperate moments.

On this day, may you turn to me in your moments of despair, knowing that I am always ready to offer help and healing. Amen.


# 9 April

Today, let's reflect on the story of Matthew's call (Matthew 9:9-13). Matthew was a tax collector, despised by many. Yet I chose him to be one of my disciples.

This story shows that no one is unworthy of my love or grace. Whatever your past, I invite you to follow me and enter into a relationship with me.

On this day, remember that you are precious in my eyes and that I am calling you to draw close to me, regardless of your past. Amen.

# 10 April

Today I invite you to meditate on the story of the Samaritan woman at the well (John 4:1-26). Despite her past mistakes and cultural differences, I offered her living water, a new life in me.

This story reminds us that no one is excluded from my grace and love. I come for everyone, regardless of our past or our cultural differences.

On this day, may you know that you are worthy of my love and my grace. May you accept the living water I offer you, a life renewed in me. Amen.

# 11 April

Today, think about the story of the healing of the ten lepers (Luke 17:11-19). I healed ten lepers, but only one came back to thank me for the blessing he had received.

This story reminds us of the importance of being grateful to God for all his blessings, large and small.

On this day, may you recognise the many ways in which God blesses you, and take the time to express your gratitude. May your life be filled with sincere gratitude. Amen.

# 12 April

Today, reflect on the story of the healing of the man with the withered hand (Mark 3:1-6). Despite criticism and danger, I chose to heal this man on the Sabbath, affirming the value of compassion and love over strict observance of the rules.

This story reminds us that love and compassion must always take precedence over rules and traditions.

On this day, may you be filled with compassion for those around you, and may your love reflect my love for you. May you choose love and compassion, even when it goes against the expectations of others. Amen.

# 13 April

Today, let's reflect on the story of Jairus' daughter (Mark 5:21-43). Despite the report of her death, I revived Jairus' daughter, showing that nothing is impossible for me.

This story reminds us that even in the most desperate situations, I have the power to turn circumstances around and bring life.

On this day, I pray that you will trust in my power and my ability to work in your life, even when things seem impossible. May you have the assurance of my presence and power in every situation. Amen.

# 14 April

Today, let's reflect on the story of the healing of the deaf and dumb man (Mark 7:31-37). Despite communication barriers, I touched and healed this man, opening his ears and mouth.

This story reminds us that I am capable of healing and overcoming any obstacle that comes our way.

On this day, may you have confidence in my ability to heal and transform your life. May you know that I am at work in every situation, even those that seem impossible. Amen.

# 15 April

Today, I suggest you meditate on the story of the encounter with the rich young man (Matthew 19:16-22). Despite his wealth, this young man was dissatisfied. I showed him that there was one thing he needed to be truly happy: to give up his possessions and follow me.

This story invites us to reflect on what is really important in life.

Today, look around you, beyond your material possessions. Look for true wealth in me, in my teachings and in the love you give and receive. May this day bring you even closer to me. Amen.

# 16 April

Today, let's reflect on the story of the vine and the branches (John 15:1-8). I am the true vine and you are the branches. Without me, you can do nothing.

This story reminds us of our constant dependence on me for our spiritual growth and effectiveness.

On this day, may you remain connected to me, finding your strength and purpose in me. May you bear much fruit for my glory, demonstrating love, joy, peace, patience, kindness, faithfulness, gentleness and self-control. Amen.


# 17 April

As the sun rises, remember that I'm always with you. Every moment, every challenge you face, know that I'm there, supporting and guiding you. I offer you strength to overcome every trial, wisdom to light your way, and love to fill your heart. Let the peace I give soothe your worries and calm your fears.

On this day, look around you and find the little joys that dot your path. May you be a reflection of my love to those around you, bringing comfort and hope to their lives. Let your light shine and touch those who need it.

Look to me for the source of your peace, strength and love. Remember that you are precious to me and that I cherish you. May this day be filled with blessings, joy and fulfilment. May your heart be light and your spirit serene, knowing that I am by your side. Amen.

# 18 April

On this day, I invite you to look at the world with eyes full of gratitude. Every moment, every interaction, every breath is a precious gift. May you appreciate the beauty of a sunrise, the sweetness of a shared smile, the comfort of a kind word.

As you go about your day, let gratitude fill your heart and light your way. May you see my blessings in the big and small things that make up your daily life. May this gratitude enrich your life, strengthen your faith and bring joy to those around you.

Together, we face every challenge, every opportunity. May you remember that you are never alone and that my love for you is unconditional and eternal. May this day be filled with gratitude, joy and love. Amen.

# 19 April

On this day, I invite you to explore the depths of your own heart, the place where I dwell within you. May you connect to this inner source of love, compassion and wisdom. May you recognise your own potential and innate worth.

Don't forget that you are capable of great things, that you can bring a brilliant light to this world. May you remember that I'm with you, supporting and guiding you every step of the way.

Today, let your inner light shine. Open your heart to love, generosity and understanding. May you touch the lives of others with kindness and compassion, reflecting my love in you. May your day be filled with fulfilment and peace. Amen.

# 20 April

Today, I ask you to turn towards nature and see in it the reflection of my creation. Every tree, every flower, every river is a manifestation of my love for the world. May you cherish this earth that is your home, respecting and protecting it as a precious gift. Let the beauty of nature remind you of my infinite love for you and for all creation. May you see in every sunrise a new opportunity, and in every sunset the promise of peace.

Never forget that you are part of this wonderful creation. Your love, compassion and kindness can make all the difference in the world. May you go forward today with respect and gratitude for the earth and all that it harbours. May your day be blessed with beauty, peace and joy. Amen.

# 21 April

Today, I'm asking you to practise patience, a virtue that is often forgotten, yet so precious. In the face of turmoil, annoyance or uncertainty, may you find the serenity to wait, to listen and to understand.

Patience is not passivity, but a quiet strength that enables you to see more clearly, to show compassion and to act wisely. It is calm in the midst of storm, confidence in the expectation of spring.

As you go through this day, may you carry this patience within you. Let it soften your words, guide your actions, soothe your spirit. Remember that I am with you, in your moments of haste and in your moments of rest. May your day be sweet and full of peace. Amen.

## 22 April

Today I invite you to contemplate the power of forgiveness. This gesture of love, sometimes difficult to offer, is a key to healing and freedom. May you find the strength to forgive others and yourself for the mistakes of the past.

Forgiveness is not oblivion, but a way of accepting and releasing pain to make way for love and peace. It allows you to see wounds as lessons, to transform suffering into wisdom.

As you go through this day, may you welcome forgiveness into your heart. Let it heal your wounds, renew your spirit, restore your soul. Remember that I am with you, guiding you on this path of healing. May your day be filled with reconciliation, liberation and love. May your day be filled with reconciliation, liberation and love. Amen.

## 23 April

Today I'm asking you to open your heart to the beauty of humility. It doesn't mean devaluing yourself, but acknowledging your strengths and weaknesses with disarming sincerity. May you accept yourself as you are, knowing that you are loved and precious in my eyes. Humility invites you to listen rather than talk, to learn rather than judge, to give without expecting anything in return. It is the silent wisdom that reminds you to see others as your equals, to honour life in all its forms.

As you go about your day, let humility guide your actions. May you walk this earth with gentleness, respecting others in their uniqueness, and loving yourself with kindness. May your day be full of simplicity, respect and authenticity. We pray Amen.

## 24 April

On this day, I invite you to reflect on the importance of faith. Faith is not an immutable certainty, but an evolving trust in my love for you. May you feel this divine presence in every moment, every trial, every triumph.

Faith is the anchor that holds you through the storm, the star that guides your path through the darkness. It reminds you that you are never alone, that I am with you every step of the way.

Today, let faith light up your heart. May you have confidence in life, in yourself, in my eternal love. May your day be filled with courage, serenity and deep trust. Amen.

## 25 April

On this day, I invite you to meditate on the art of listening. To truly listen is to open your heart to others, to recognise their humanity as much as your own. May you become a comforting presence for those who need to be heard.

Listening is a silent form of love. It invites you to suspend your judgements, to withhold your advice, to simply be there, in a caring presence. It reminds you that every voice counts, that every story deserves to be respected.

As you live this day, may you practice authentic listening. Let it soften your interactions, deepen your relationships, enrich your understanding of the world. Remember that I am with you, always listening with love and patience. May your day be filled with compassion, respect and true connection. May your day be filled with compassion, respect and true connection. Amen.

# 26 April

Today I invite you to think about kindness. Kindness is not just an action, but a state of being that emanates from your heart and spreads out into the world. May you let your heart open and pour out this goodness to everyone you meet.

Kindness is a bridge that links hearts, a balm that soothes pain. It is a light that shines in the darkness, a hand held out in solitude. It reminds you that love is the most powerful force in the universe.

As you go through this day, let kindness guide you. May you act with kindness, speak with tenderness, and think with love. May your day be filled with gentleness, generosity and compassion. Amen.


# 27 April

On this day, I invite you to contemplate the power of silence. Silence is not just the absence of noise, but a peaceful presence that invites you to listen more deeply, to perceive reality more clearly. May you find a moment of silence today, and let it nourish you.

Silence is an inner sanctuary, a place of renewal and peace. It gives you space to listen to your heart, to welcome your emotions, to connect with your divine essence.

As you live this day, let silence be your companion. May you rejoice in these quiet moments, and let their wisdom guide you. May your day be filled with tranquillity, clarity and deep peace. Amen.

## 28 April

Today I invite you to celebrate the miracle of life. Every moment is a gift, every breath a blessing. May you marvel at the beauty of creation, from the smallest grain of sand to the immensity of the universe.

Life is a wonderful journey, a constant dance of light and shadow, joy and pain. It is a testament to my love for you, a call to love in return.

As you live this day, let yourself be moved by the miracle of life. May you cherish every moment, every encounter, every lesson learned. May your day be filled with wonder, gratitude and love. Amen.

## 29 April

Today, I'd like to take a look at the idea of curiosity. Curiosity is not an intrusion, but an openness of mind, a desire to learn and discover. May you keep an open mind and continually marvel at the universe around you.

Curiosity is a compass that guides you towards the unknown, a key that opens the doors to knowledge. It allows you to grow and evolve, to stay young at heart and young at heart.

As you go about your day, embrace curiosity. May you ask questions, seek answers, and marvel at the mysteries of life. May your day be filled with discovery, learning and wonder. Amen.

## April 30th

Today I invite you to reflect on the importance of generosity. Generosity is not just a question of material gifts, but a state of mind that is happy to share, to give without expecting anything in return. May you cultivate this generosity in your heart.

Generosity is a ray of sunshine on a cloudy day, a source of water in a desert. It enriches not only those who receive it, but above all those who give it.

As you live this day, let generosity be your guide. May you give with joy, share with love, and contribute to the beauty of this world. May your day be filled with abundance, sharing and love. Amen.

## 1st May

Today, let me talk to you about the joy of creation. Whether through art, work or the simple expression of your thoughts, every act of creation is a celebration of life and love.

Creation is an echo of the universe, a dance of the spirit. It is an affirmation of your power, a manifestation of your freedom.

As you go about your day, embrace the joy of creation. May you create with love, express with boldness, and contribute to the beauty of this world. May your day be filled with creativity, inspiration and wonder. Amen.

# 2 May

Today, consider the importance of wisdom. Wisdom is not just the accumulation of knowledge, but the ability to apply it wisely in life. May you seek wisdom and let it light your way.

Wisdom is a light in the darkness, a sure guide in the maze of life. It helps you to make the right choices, to discern truth from falsehood, good from evil.

As you go about your day, aspire to wisdom. May you think before you act, listen before you speak, understand before you judge. May your day be illuminated by wisdom, understanding and insight. Amen.

# 3 May

Today I'd like you to reflect on the idea of adaptability. Adaptability is not compromise, but the flexibility needed to evolve with life's changes. May you embrace adaptability and allow it to strengthen you.

Adaptability is a breeze that moves with the wind, a river that bypasses obstacles. It keeps you moving, finding new solutions, seeing possibilities where others see dead ends.

As the day unfolds, be adaptable. May you embrace change with an open mind, show resilience in the face of adversity, and transform yourself to become the best version of yourself. May your day be filled with growth, discovery and resilience. Amen.

# 4 May

On this day, I remind you of the words of the holy apostle Paul in his letter to the Corinthians, "Where the Spirit of the Lord is, there is freedom". (2 Corinthians 3:17). On this day, may you rediscover that freedom, the freedom that invites you to let go and welcome the unexpected with confidence and serenity.

The freedom of the Spirit calls you to spontaneity, to the ability to marvel at every moment, every encounter, as if for the first time. It's an invitation to dance with life, to let the wind of the Spirit guide you, without seeking to control, without fearing the unpredictable.

So, on this day, may the Spirit of the Lord breathe into you, freeing you from your fears and inviting you to be spontaneous. May your day be a hymn to freedom, a dance with the unexpected, a love song to life. Amen.

# 5 May

I think today of the story of Mary of Bethany, the woman who, with a generous heart, poured precious perfume on my feet. A spontaneous and extravagant gesture of love and devotion. May her story inspire and encourage you to love generously and without reserve.

Mary did not count the cost of her love; she did not hesitate in the face of other people's opinions. She simply acted, guided by her heart, as a sign of gratitude and love. This is an example of what truly free love can be.

May you, on this day, follow the example of Mary of Bethany. May you love boldly, generously, without calculation or hesitation. May your day be blessed with love, generosity and spontaneity. Amen.

# 6 May

Today I'd like to share with you the story of Saint Francis of Assisi, who gave up a life of wealth to live in simplicity. He teaches us a valuable lesson about the value of simplicity and detachment from material possessions.

Saint Francis found joy and freedom not in the accumulation of goods, but in the simplicity of life, in the love of nature and in service to those in need. He reminds us that true wealth is found in the heart, not in the wallet. Today, may you remember the example of Saint Francis. May you find joy in the simple things, and wealth in the love and kindness you share with others. May your day be blessed with simplicity, generosity and joy. Amen.

# 7 May

On this day, I am reminded of the parable of the sower, who scattered his seeds on different types of soil. This story illustrates the importance of opening our hearts to welcome the Word with joy and allow it to bear fruit. Some seeds fall on the path, on the stone, among the thorns, and others on good soil. Each type of soil represents a different disposition of our heart to the Word of God. Only good soil, an open and receptive heart, can allow the Word to take root and grow.

On this day, may you prepare the soil of your heart to be like good earth. May you welcome the Word with an open heart, ready to change and grow. May your day be filled with growth, transformation and new understanding. Amen.

# 8th May

On this day, I turn to the example of Mary Magdalene, who was the first to see the risen Christ. Her devotion and love for me were not diminished by her sadness. She stayed, weeping, even when all the others had left the tomb. Her faithfulness was rewarded by the first appearance of the Resurrection.

Mary Magdalene teaches us the importance of remaining faithful, even in times of pain and despair. She reminds us that it is often in our darkest moments that the light of the Resurrection is most felt.

On this day, may you remember the faithfulness of Mary Magdalene. Even in your moments of sadness, may you remain open to the presence of divine love and light. May your day be blessed with perseverance and hope. Amen.

# 9 May

Today I turn to the symbol of water. In the Bible, water is often used as an image of renewal and purification, of life and growth. Water is essential to life, just as my presence is essential to your spiritual life.

As water enlivens the desert and transforms it into a flourishing garden, so my presence in you can transform your heart and your life. Do not let the cares of the world dry you up and make you barren, but rather look to me for the source of living water that refreshes and gives life. On this day, may you remember the water that gives life. May you turn to me for refreshment and renewal. May your day be blessed with growth and transformation. Amen.

# 10 May

Today I contemplate the patience of my servant Job, who despite trials and adversity, never lost faith in me. His story reminds us that life's difficulties are not a sign of my absence, but an invitation to a deeper trust.

Like Job, be resilient in times of adversity. May your faith not be shaken by trials, but refined and strengthened, like gold purified by fire.

On this day, may you find in yourself the patience and resilience of Job. May you find in every difficulty an opportunity to grow in faith and trust. May your day be blessed with strength and perseverance. Amen.

# 11 May

Today, let us reflect on the life of the apostle Peter. Despite his denial, he was forgiven and restored. Peter, an impulsive and passionate man, was transformed by my love into a strong and dedicated leader of my church.

Her journey is a reminder that even when you fall, I'm there to pick you up again. Past mistakes don't have to define your future. Love and forgiveness can transform your heart and guide you towards a new goal.

On this day, may you receive the grace of transformation, like Peter. May your past mistakes be forgiven, and may you be guided along a path of renewal. May your day be blessed with reconciliation and restoration. Amen.

# 12 May

Today we remember Saint Francis of Assisi, known for his love of the poor and of nature. His dedication to living according to the Gospel was so profound that he renounced all material possessions to devote himself fully to my service and that of humanity.

Saint Francis reminds us of the importance of simplicity, generosity and humility. On this day, I invite you to turn to these virtues. May you find joy in simplicity, fulfilment in generosity, and strength in humility.

On this day, may you remember the life of Saint Francis of Assisi. May his example inspire you to live a simpler, more generous and more humble life. May your day be blessed with peace and contentment. Amen.

# 13 May

Today, let's reflect on the story of the apostle Paul. Paul, once a fervent persecutor of Christians, was transformed by my grace into a fervent defender of the faith. His story is a powerful illustration of how my grace can transform even the most hardened of hearts.

May you remember Paul when you feel far from me or when you doubt your ability to change. Know that my grace is enough for you, that it can reach you where you are and transform you from within.

On this day, may you experience my transforming grace, just as Paul did. May your day be blessed with redemption and renewal. Amen.

# 14 May

On this day, I invite you to consider the life of Saint Thérèse of Lisieux, often called the "little flower". Despite her short life, she left a lasting legacy through her "little way" of love and simplicity.

Her conviction was that it is not necessary to do great deeds to show love, but that small deeds done with love are of great value. Thérèse reminds us that every act of kindness, no matter how small, contributes to the greater work of love in the world.

On this day, may you adopt the "little way" of Saint Thérèse. May every small act of kindness you perform today be imbued with love. May your day be blessed with simplicity and love. Amen.

# 15 May

On this day, let us meditate on Saint John the evangelist, the apostle of love. John always emphasised the centrality of love in the Christian life. He reminds us that "God is love" and that he who loves knows God.

John invites us to love not just in words, but in deeds and in truth. May your love not only be a feeling, but may it manifest itself in concrete actions of kindness towards others.

On this day, may you be inspired by Saint John to live authentic love. May you love not only in word, but in deed and in truth. May your day be blessed with true love. Amen.

# 16 May

Today, let's consider the example of Saint Thomas, the apostle who doubted, but in the end affirmed his faith in me with strength and clarity. Thomas shows us that even in our doubts and uncertainties, we can always return to the truth of my presence.

Saint Thomas invites us to seek answers, to ask questions, and to never stop searching for the truth. He reminds us that faith is not blind acceptance, but a constant quest to understand and love more.

On this day, may you embrace Thomas's questioning spirit. May your doubts and questions take you further on your journey of faith, and lead you to a deeper understanding of my love for you. May your day be blessed with quest and discovery. Amen.

# 17 May

Today I invite you to meditate on Saint Matthew, the publican who became an apostle. He gave up his past life to follow me, proving that no one is beyond the reach of my mercy.

Matthew reminds us that everyone is invited to the Lord's table, whatever their background. He invites us to abandon our old ways and follow the path of light and love.

On this day, may the example of Matthew guide you. May you remember that you are always loved, whatever your past.

# 18 May

Today I invite you to reflect on the story of Saint John the Evangelist, my beloved disciple. John, who faithfully remained by my side until the end, gives us an example of true friendship and dedication.

Saint John reminds us that love is the essence of my word. He invites us to love others as I have loved you, unconditionally and without judgement.

On this day, may you live with the tenderness and love of John. May you share this love with those who cross your path. May your day be blessed with unconditional love and faithful devotion. Amen.

# 19 May

Let us reflect today on the beauty of creation, the song of the birds, the rustle of the trees, the majestic mountains and the deep oceans. They are all a testament to the wonder of existence and the greatness of my love for you.

Nature reminds us that every little thing is sacred. It invites us to respect and care for our Earth, our common home.

On this day, may the beauty of creation inspire and guide you. May you remember to honour and cherish every aspect of this magnificent planet. May your day be blessed by the singing of birds and the rustling of leaves in the wind. Amen.

# 20 May

Today, I invite you to meditate on the story of the Samaritan woman who, despite her sins, was touched by my word and transformed her life. She became an example of conversion and evangelisation, bringing the good news to her people.

The Samaritan woman reminds us that no one is beyond the reach of my grace, that everyone can find salvation and renewal. She invites us to share the joy of the Gospel with those around us.

May today be a day for reflection and sharing. May you be a source of hope for those you meet, just as the Samaritan woman was for her people. Amen.

# 21 May

On this day, I invite you to meditate on the importance of humility. Think of Saint Francis of Assisi, who gave up a life of comfort and luxury to live in simplicity and poverty, dedicated to serving those most in need.

The example of Saint Francis invites us to set aside our selfish desires and embrace selfless love. He reminds us that it is by lowering ourselves that we rise, by serving others that we come closer to the divine.

May this day be one of humility and service. May you remember that the greatest rewards often come from the smallest acts of love. Amen.

## 22 May

On this day, remember that in every daily challenge lies an opportunity to learn and grow. The traffic jams that test your patience, the misunderstandings that challenge your sense of compassion, the setbacks that demand your resilience - these moments are blessings in disguise.

Remember that the glass can be seen as half empty or half full. It's a question of perspective. May you always choose to see the good in every situation, to find gratitude in every day.

May every human experience teach you love, humility, patience and faith. And may each step bring you closer to me, finding peace and serenity in my presence. May my grace be your strength this day. Amen.

## 23 May

On this day, remember that in every human interaction, you have the opportunity to be a reflection of my love. Every smile you offer, every word of encouragement you speak, every act of kindness you do, can bring light into someone's life.

Know that you are never alone in your trials. Through the compassion and kindness of others, I am there. Likewise, in your compassion and kindness towards others, I am present.

May you find the strength to be a source of love and light for those around you. May your day be filled with moments of grace and kindness, and may you feel my love in every moment. May you feel my love in every moment. Amen.

## 24 May

Today, remember that every job you do is an opportunity to serve with love and integrity. Whether it's a humble job or a great responsibility, every effort you make is important and precious in my eyes.

Your daily work, whether in education, health, business or the home, is a form of prayer when it is done with a sincere heart and pure intention. That's how you transform ordinary acts into extraordinary ones.

Today, may you find joy in your work, see its value and importance, and do it with all your heart as you do it for me. May your day be filled with rewarding accomplishments and may peace and contentment be with you. May peace and contentment be with you. Amen.


## 25 May

On this day, may you find the courage to forgive yourself for any mistakes you may have made. Like a child learning to walk, every fall is part of the learning process. Your mistakes don't define you, they guide you in becoming a better version of yourself.

Remember that I'm always here, welcoming you with open arms, ready to forgive and renew. May you be granted the same grace and mercy.

On this day, I pray that you will remember your inestimable value, forgive yourself and embrace yourself with compassion and love. May peace fill your heart and guide your steps. Amen.

# 26 May

On this day, I remind you that silence can be a prayer. In the hustle and bustle of everyday life, it can seem difficult to find calm, yet it is in these moments of silence that you can find me.

Silence isn't empty, it's full of answers. Take the time today to sit quietly, concentrate on your breathing and listen to the silence. You'll find peace, inspiration and wisdom.

I wish you a day of calm and serenity, wherever you are, whatever you're doing. May the peace you find in silence accompany you throughout your day. Amen.

# 27 May

Today I'd like to remind you of the importance of self-esteem. It's the foundation of your relationship with yourself and others. As you love yourself, you also love others.

May this day bring you a deep awareness of your intrinsic value. You are unique, you are precious, you are worthy of love and respect. Don't devalue yourself, don't neglect yourself, love yourself as I love you.

Today, I wish you to love yourself with kindness and compassion, to celebrate yourself with joy and gratitude, and to radiate this love to everyone you meet. Amen.

## 28 May

On this day, I invite you to observe the beauty of the natural world around you. Every flower, every tree, every stream is a testimony to creation, a reflection of God's love.

I remind you that you too are part of this wonderful creation. So when you appreciate the beauty of nature, you also recognise the beauty within yourself.

I pray that you can find comfort in nature, feel connected to everything around you and sense the divine presence in everything. May this day bring you closer to creation, and through it, to your Creator. Amen.

## 29 May

Today, I encourage you to embrace challenges. Remember, it's through trials that we build character and develop perseverance.

I remind you that you are never alone in these moments. I'm with you, guiding and supporting you, even if sometimes you can't see it.

I pray that you will have the strength to face the challenges of this day with courage and resilience. May every obstacle you encounter be an opportunity for you to grow and get closer to your true nature. Amen.

## 30th May

Today, I invite you to be humble. It's a virtue that's often misunderstood, but it's essential. Humility does not mean considering ourselves inferior, but recognising our strengths and limitations with truth and simplicity.

In humility you find a clear perspective and a path to wisdom. It helps you live with gratitude, learn from others and accept help when you need it.

I pray that this day will help you to embrace humility, to recognise your interdependence with others and with the world around you, to remember that you are a precious part of the greater whole. Amen.

## 31 May

On this last day of May, I'd like to remind you of the importance of renewal. Like the changing seasons, it's normal and healthy to evolve, grow and change.

Don't be afraid of endings, because every ending heralds a new beginning. Let go of what is no longer necessary and welcome the new with open arms.

I pray that you will be able to face change with confidence and faith, knowing that every step of your life is guided by infinite love. May this day bring you the serenity to accept the past, the strength to live the present and the hope to welcome the future. Amen.

# 1st June

As we enter a new month, I invite you to reflect. Take a moment to look back and assess your progress, successes and challenges.

Don't judge yourself harshly, but embrace your experiences with compassion and understanding. It's by understanding where you've been that you can determine where you want to go.

I pray that you find wisdom in your reflection, and that you can use what you've learned to move forward with courage and confidence. May each day of the new month be a new opportunity to learn, grow and become the best version of yourself. Amen.

# 2 June

On this day, I invite you to contemplate the power of love. Not just romantic love, but love in all its forms: family love, brotherly love, self-love, love for creation, love for humanity.

Love is a force that can transform, heal and unify. It gives courage, calms fears and builds bridges where there are gaps.

I pray that you will feel the love that is within you and around you, that you will give it freely and welcome it without reservation. May love be your guide, your comfort and your strength this day and all the days to come. Amen.

# 3 June

Today I invite you to reflect on the notion of sacrifice. Sacrifice, in its purest sense, is an act of love. It is an expression of love for others, a willingness to give up something for the good of others.

Remember that, as I did on the cross, sacrifice can be a path to true love and transformation. It's not a burden, but an opportunity to show compassion, generosity and kindness.

I pray that you will have the courage to make the sacrifices necessary for the good of others and for your own spiritual growth. May your love for others be shown through your actions and sacrifices. Amen.

# 4 June

Today I want to encourage you to seek the truth. The world may be full of confusion, misinformation and uncertainty, but at the heart of it all, the truth remains.

Remember that it's important to seek the truth, not only in the outside world, but also within yourself. Your inner truth is your guide, your north. It is unique to you and precious.

I pray that you will have the wisdom to discern the truth, the strength to defend it and the courage to live by it. May truth be your light and your guide in times of darkness. Amen.

# 5 June

On this day, I invite you to focus on generosity. Just as the sun gives generously of its light and warmth to the earth, may you also give generously of yourself to others.

I pray that you will recognise the opportunities to give, whether it's your time, your love or your support. May your heart be open and ready to share what you have with those in need.

Seek to be a source of light in the lives of others, just as the sun is for the earth. May your generosity blossom and intensify, bringing joy and satisfaction not only to those you help, but also to yourself. Amen.

# 6 June

Today I'd like to encourage you to focus on patience. There is wisdom in waiting for the right moment, just as the farmer waits patiently for his seeds to germinate and grow.

I pray that you will develop the patience to get through the difficult times in your life, that you will learn to see the beauty of the process and the reward that comes with time.

That you accept that everything happens in its own time, and that you don't rush into things, but wait with confidence and serenity. For as Ecclesiastes says: "There is a time for everything". Amen.

# 7 June

Today, let's look at humility, the virtue that lifts souls. May you remember, like the lilies of the field, the beauty in simplicity and the greatness in humility.

I pray that you will not lose yourself in the pride of your achievements, but that you will recognise the hand of God in everything you do. That you understand that every success, every talent, every ability is a gift that has been entrusted to you.

Love with a humble heart, serve with humble hands, and walk the path of life with humble feet. Humility is the foundation of wisdom, and it opens the door to true greatness. Amen.

# 8 June

On this day, let us reflect on perseverance. Like the little seed that grows through the hard earth to reach the sunlight, you too are called to persevere through life's challenges.

I pray that you will find the strength to keep going, even when things seem impossible. That you won't give up, even when you don't immediately see the fruits of your efforts.

Remember that every step you take, however small, brings you closer to your goal. May you be sustained in perseverance and hope, knowing that all work done with love and determination bears fruit in its own time. Amen.

# 9 June

On this day, I invite you to contemplate the joy that exists in every moment. Joy is not only present in great moments of triumph, but also in the little things of everyday life.

I pray that you will be able to see the joy in a shared smile, a kind word, an act of kindness. May you be able to find joy even in difficult times, remembering that every trial is an opportunity to grow and become stronger.

Remember that joy is not a fleeting state, but a way of seeing the world. May you live each day with joy in your heart, grateful for every blessing, every moment of beauty and every gesture of love. Amen.

# 10 June

Today I'd like to encourage you to open up to the wisdom that lies in silence. In our busy, noisy world, silence can sometimes seem frightening, but it's in silence that we can really hear.

I hope you find the courage to be silent, to listen to your heart and to the whispers of life around you. That you will discover the wisdom that lies not only in words, but also in quiet moments.

I guide you to turn to silence with courage, so that you can hear the truths that are not always expressed, but are always present. May you find peace, comfort and clarity in silence. Amen.

# 11 June

Today I'm asking you to look at life's challenges. Don't see them as obstacles, but as opportunities to grow, mature and draw closer to me. When the storm rages, remember that I am your refuge.

Every trial, every difficulty, is an opportunity to learn and gain wisdom. May you find the strength to face these moments with courage and perseverance. Fear not, for I am always at your side, offering you my help and my love.

When you feel the weight of the world on your shoulders, may you remember that I carry that weight with you. Don't be overwhelmed, but let me guide you through the storms of life. Amen.

# 12 June

Dear child, remember the parable of the sower. Like the seed on the rock, you can feel rootless, swept away by the winds of adversity. Like the seed among the thorns, you may feel suffocated by the cares of this world. But, dear child, aspire to be the seed in the good soil, which, despite the challenges, bears fruit with patience. May you always find the strength to persevere, to grow and to prosper in the richness of My love for you. Amen.

# 13 June

Let your heart be like a lamp, dear child. Do not let it be darkened by fear or doubt. Remember Me, your guide in the darkness. I am the lighthouse that shines in the night, the watchman who makes sure you don't stumble. Even in the darkest moments, I am with you. I'm the morning star, the light before dawn, the sure sign that a new day is approaching. May you always find the light in Me, and may that light guide you along the path of peace and love. May your trust in Me illuminate your days and nights, giving your heart the warmth of an unshakeable flame. Amen.

# 14 June

In this hectic life, I invite you to seek silence. In silence, you will find serenity and the space to hear My voice. I am in the murmur of the wind, the hum of the stream and the silence of the night. Don't forget that in silence you come closer to Me, to the divine mystery. Make silence your sanctuary, a place where you can rest and recharge your batteries. Allow tranquillity to soothe your mind and heart, and in that peace discover the true love I have for you. Let silence be your guide, your friend, your consolation. In silence you will never be alone, for I will always be there. Embrace the silence, my child, and let it bring you closer to Me. Amen.

## 15 June

Today I'm talking to you about wonder. Wonder is the beginning of wisdom. Look at the world with the eyes of wonder, like a child discovering creation for the first time. Contemplate the stars in the night sky, observe the beauty of a simple butterfly, listen to the song of the birds at dawn. All these wonders are gifts for you. Through wonder, you open yourself up to the presence of the infinite in the finite, the divine in the ordinary. Wonder allows you to perceive my presence in everything. So always keep wonder in your heart, for it is the path that leads to Me. Amen.

## 16 June

Today, I'm talking to you about the impulse of the heart. The impulse of the heart is the expression of your deep love for others, for creation, for Me. It manifests itself in your desire to help, to support, to console. When you act from the heart, you bear witness to the love that lives within you. It's a genuine love, without expectations, simply given. Love from the heart, and you'll see that you'll receive much more in return. This love will circulate between you and others, and every gesture, every word, every look will be opportunities to share this love. Amen.

# 17 June

My child, I'm talking to you today about perseverance. Sometimes you may feel exhausted, as if every step required an immense effort. But remember that the biggest oak tree began as a small seed. It took time, patience and, above all, perseverance to grow to its full size. So don't despair when you encounter obstacles along the way. Every trial is an opportunity for you to grow, to become stronger. Never give up, even when the path seems too difficult. Know that I am with you every step of the way. Amen.

# 18 June

My child, today I'm talking to you about humility. In a world that glorifies visible success, I invite you to seek the inner triumph of humility. Like John the Baptist who said, "He must increase and I must decrease". By diminishing yourself, you leave more room for my divine presence in you. Humility is not weakness, but the strength to recognise your limits and open yourself up to My grace. When you are humble, you acknowledge your dependence on Me, and you open the door to my infinite power. So remain humble, for it is in humility that you will find your true greatness. Amen.

# 20 June

Let us meditate on the idea of sharing. Sharing is not just an act of giving something material, it is an act of love, generosity and humanity. When you share, you recognise that what you have is a gift from Me, and you choose to give it back willingly. Sharing brings you closer to Me, because it teaches you compassion, empathy and love for your neighbour. Always look for opportunities to share, not because it's an obligation, but because it's a joy. Amen.

# 21 June

Remember that every moment of everyday life is an opportunity to draw closer to Me. In your work, find dignity and the opportunity to serve others. In your health, give thanks for the gift of life and do everything you can to preserve it. In your family, love and be loved, for it is there that you learn the first lessons of love and sacrifice. With your friends, find comfort, encouragement and joy. These aspects of daily life are all opportunities for you to live My Word and show My love in the world. Amen.

## 22 June

In moments of doubt and uncertainty, don't forget that strength is within you. Whether you have to make decisions at work or face a personal challenge, remember that I have given you an unshakeable will. Go forward with courage, with faith in your ability to overcome obstacles. Pray that this strength will be guided by wisdom and compassion, so that your actions in the world will be a reflection of My divine will. And never forget that you are never alone in these challenges - I am by your side, supporting and guiding you. When you feel exhausted or overwhelmed, find comfort in My presence. May your days be filled with peace, joy and love, gifts I've made available for you to discover and share.

## 23 June

When you're in good health, it's easy to forget how precious life is. Take the time today to give thanks for the gift of health. Whether you're taking a walk, enjoying a meal or simply breathing, every moment is a reminder of your body's wonderful ability to experience the world. Take care of this body, for it is the vessel that allows you to live and love in this world. At the same time, I'm here for you in times of illness and pain. You are never alone. Take a moment to feel My presence with you now, and know that you are loved.

## 24 June

Today, remember that your work, whatever its nature, has meaning. You contribute to the world in many ways, even if you don't always see it. Through your work, you touch the lives of others, you bring change, you bring joy, knowledge, assistance, beauty. Remember that every task, big or small, has its value. Even when you're tired or discouraged, know that I'm by your side. Do your best, and know that your efforts are never in vain. Do each task with love, because love transforms everything it touches.

## 25 June

Know that your health is a great blessing, a precious gift to be cherished and preserved. Remember that taking care of your body also means taking care of your mind. Sleep, a healthy diet, exercise - all these things contribute to your overall well-being.

Just as you take care of your physical health, take care of your emotional and spiritual health. Nourish your mind with positive thoughts, prayer and meditation. Don't forget that I'm always here for you, ready to listen and support you.

And don't forget to laugh and have fun. Laughter is good medicine, a natural remedy that soothes the heart and mind. Look for the moments of joy, the little pleasures of everyday life. Remember that even in difficult times, there's always a reason to smile. Have respect for nature too. Walk barefoot on the grass, breathe in the fresh forest air, listen to the birds singing. Take the time to connect with the world around you. Nature is an inexhaustible source of peace and serenity.

# 26 June

Today I'm inviting you to cultivate patience with yourself and others. In a fast-paced and demanding world, it can be difficult to find the time to breathe, to refocus and to be patient. Yet patience is a precious virtue that allows us to live more serenely and deepen our relationships.

Remember that every day is an opportunity to grow and learn, even if the path sometimes seems difficult. Accept challenges calmly and serenely, and be gentle with yourself in times of difficulty.

Patience, my friend, is the key to a balanced and harmonious life. Cultivate it every day.

# 27 June

In a world full of noise, I invite you today to find a moment of silence. A moment to connect with yourself, with your own inner voice. Silence is not the absence of sound, but an opportunity to listen to what's really important.

In this silence, listen to your heart and your thoughts. Make peace with the turbulence of life, and find tranquillity in the midst of chaos. It's in these moments of silence that you can find yourself and recharge your batteries.

Silence is a little-known treasure, an oasis of tranquillity in the desert of everyday life. Find your silence, and you'll find your peace.

## 28 June

Every day offers a new beginning, an opportunity to reinvent and reimagine. The sunrise is a constant reminder that even after the darkness, the light always returns. As this new day dawns, I invite you to embrace the hope and promise it brings. Leave yesterday's mistakes behind and look to today with a fresh perspective. For every sunrise offers a blank canvas on which to paint. Remember, it's you who holds the brush. Choose the colours of your day and create your own work of art. Let each brushstroke tell a story of resilience, courage and love. As the sun rises, remember that there is always a chance to start again. Seize that chance, with the confidence that beyond every sunset lies a new dawn, a new day, a new beginning.

## 29 June

Life's challenges are not there to break us, but to shape us. Every trial is a chance to show our resilience, our courage. Like a diamond formed under pressure, you grow stronger with every battle you face.

Wear your scars proudly, because they're a symbol of your strength and perseverance. They are a testament to your courage in weathering the storms. Every mark is a sign that you've survived, that you're a fighter.

In every moment of difficulty, remember that you have the ability to choose how you react. Choose to learn, to grow and to see every challenge as an opportunity. The road may be arduous, but know that you are never alone. I'm with you, encouraging you, accompanying you every step of the way.

# 30 June

Sometimes the days can seem heavy and tiredness can overwhelm you. When you're tired, remember to turn inward and seek peace within yourself. There you'll find the rest and serenity you need.

I'm with you, ready to offer you the comfort and support you need. Take the time to recharge your batteries, because it's in this calm that you'll find the strength to carry on.

And always remember that every day is a new chance to love, to grow, to live. So welcome it with gratitude.

# 1st July

The start of a new month brings unexplored promise. Where you see challenges, see opportunities to grow. Where you see the unknown, see the potential for new discoveries.

Never forget that every experience is a valuable lesson, and every interaction is an opportunity to love and be loved. Be brave, embrace change, put fear aside and move forward with confidence.

In every moment of this new month, remember that I'm here, guiding your steps, supporting your efforts. Go forward with faith, with hope, knowing that you are never alone in your quest.

## 2 July

Today, think about the value of patience. In a fast-paced world, it's easy to get lost in the rush. But remember, everything has its time, and every process its rhythm.

The most beautiful flowers don't bloom overnight. They require patience and care, just like your spiritual and emotional growth. Don't be afraid of expectations, because they prepare you to fully appreciate the blessings that are on the way.

Take a moment today to breathe deeply, to slow down, to recognise the beauty of the present moment. Patience will teach you to cherish every step of the journey, not just the destination.

## 3 July

On this day, reflect on the power of kindness. You don't always have to be the strongest, the fastest or the smartest. Sometimes what the world needs is your kindness.

It may sometimes seem to you that kindness is a weakness, especially in a world where harshness is often rewarded. But the truth is that kindness is a courageous act of rebellion. It defies cynicism, apathy and selfishness. It shows that there is always room for love and compassion.

So today, show kindness to those you meet. You never know what battles they are fighting in silence. Your kindness could be the light they need to get through the darkness.

## 4th July

Today I invite you to think about patience. In a fast-paced world where immediacy is often expected, patience may seem out of reach. But it's a virtue you need to achieve real success and to anchor yourself in the present moment.

Patience is not just passive waiting. It is an active waiting, a gentle and determined perseverance. It asks you to embrace the process, to trust in the natural order of things and to believe that good things come to those who know how to wait.

So take the time to be patient today, whether it's with yourself, with others or with the situations in your life. Know that each moment has its own rhythm, and that sometimes the greatest blessing is to learn to wait.

## 5 July

Let's look today at the virtue of honesty. Honesty towards yourself and others is one of the most solid foundations on which to build your life. It enables clear communication, mutual trust, and nurtures your personal integrity. Being honest doesn't just mean telling the truth, it also means living your truth. It means knowing your values, respecting your limits and living in accordance with what you deeply believe. Honesty encourages you to be authentic and to express what you really feel.

Today I ask you to practise honesty in all its forms. You will find that truth is a light that dispels the shadows of uncertainty and doubt, guiding you along the path to peace and inner satisfaction.

# 6 July

Today I invite you to reflect on the gift of patience. Patience is an essential aspect of love, compassion and understanding for ourselves and others. It is the ability to tolerate obstacles, frustrations and disappointments.

Patience is not passivity or giving up, but a quiet strength that unfolds in the midst of turmoil. It allows you to stay anchored in the present moment, to resist rushing and to take the time to respond rather than react. On this day, I ask you to cultivate patience in your life. Whether you apply it in your work, in your relationships, or in your personal quest for growth, you'll discover that patience is a pillar of serenity and wisdom.

# 7 July

On this day, I remind you of part of my earthly journey, when I was in the Garden of Gethsemane, on the eve of my arrest. Stress and fear were real burdens for me in those dark hours. Yet in that moment of trial, I found the strength to say, "Not my will, but yours be done." This is not a call to abandonment or passivity, but an affirmation of trust in the Father, a trust that is also offered to you. Every day, I invite you to enter into this same spirit of trust. When life presents you with challenges, remember my night in Gethsemane and find the strength to say: "Thy will be done".

I'm with you every step of the way, every challenge you face. May you find in yourself the strength and confidence you need to let yourself be guided by the Father's will.

# 8th July

Today, I remind you of the story of the woman who touched the hem of my dress in the crowd, hoping to be healed. Her faith was so deep, so genuine, that she knew in her heart that even the smallest touch could heal her. And she was right. Her faith brought her the healing she so desperately sought. So I invite you to remember this woman when you feel exhausted or down. When you feel lost in the crowd of life, don't forget that your faith can be your guide. A simple act of faith can open the door to miracles, and I'm always there to listen to your heart and respond to your needs.

So go about your day with the faith of the woman in the crowd. Know that you are loved, that you are heard, and that healing, in all its forms, is possible for you.

# 9th July

Do you remember the meeting between Nathanael and me in John's Gospel? Nathanael was sitting under a fig tree when his friend Philip came to tell him that he had found the Messiah. Sceptical at first, Nathanael was persuaded to come and meet me. When I saw him, I recognised him, even though he had never seen me before. "Here is an Israelite of true integrity", I said, which astonished Nathanaël. How could I know who he was? I simply replied that I had seen him under the fig tree before Philip called him.

I'm telling you this to remind you that I know you too. I know your deepest thoughts, your hopes, your fears and your dreams. I watch you and I love you, even in your moments of doubt and questioning. So come, like Nathanaël, come and meet me and I'll show you even greater things.

# 10 July

Do you remember the story of the Roman centurion in Matthew's Gospel? A powerful man, commander of a hundred soldiers, yet so humble when he came to me, seeking help for his sick servant. His faith moved me. He said, "Lord, I am not worthy for you to come under my roof, but just say the word and my servant will be healed."

The centurion's faith and humility are an example to us all. That's the kind of faith I'd like you to have: a faith that is confident in my word, a faith that transcends social and cultural divisions, a faith that is humble but strong. So remember the centurion and let your faith be expressed with the same confidence and humility. For in truth, a word from me is enough to bring comfort and healing.

# 11 July

Do you remember the widow of Zarephath in the book of Kings? Despite a severe famine, she shared her last morsel of bread with my prophet Elijah. By doing this, by showing faith, she is richly blessed: her jar of oil and her jar of flour do not run dry until the famine is over.

There may be times when you feel like that widow, at the end of your tether, and yet here I am, by your side, ready to support you.

Remember the faith and generosity of the widow of Zarephath. May her story inspire you to show faith in me, even in difficult times, for I promise that you will be blessed.

# 12 July

In the Book of Judges, there is the story of Gideon, an ordinary man to whom I spoke directly, calling him a "valiant warrior". Although he doubted himself and asked for several signs to be sure of my will, he finally followed my instructions and led Israel to victory over the Midianites.

Remember Gideon when you doubt your abilities or the path to follow. Remember that I have chosen an ordinary man to do extraordinary things. Your path may seem uncertain, but rest assured that I am with you, guiding you step by step. Don't be afraid to ask for signs, to seek my presence in your life. I'm always there, supporting you through every trial and celebrating every victory with you.

# 13th July

I'd like to tell you about another lesser-known figure from the Bible: Elijah. Elijah, a man like you and me, but who prayed fervently and saw the heavens close without rain for three and a half years. It was also Elijah who challenged the prophets of Baal on Mount Carmel, showing all Israel that I am the only true God.

Never forget the power of fervent prayer and unfailing faith. Like Elijah, you can stand up courageously to challenges, even when the odds are against you, because you are never alone. I am at your side, ready to show my glory through your life. You have the potential to change the world around you through your faith and courage. Believe that and live boldly, knowing that you are loved and supported by the Lord.

## 14 July

Remember the story of Ruth in the Bible. A foreign woman, widowed and poor, who had nothing to offer, but chose to stay with her mother-in-law Naomi, even though it meant leaving her country and her family. Her devotion and loyalty to Naomi, despite her own grief and precariousness, caught my eye.

Never forget that no matter what your situation, background, wealth or social position, you have the ability to show compassion and love. You can make a significant difference in the lives of others through your actions. Kindness and faithfulness are virtues that I cherish deeply. Like Ruth, be courageous, loving and faithful, and you will find favour in my eyes.

## 15th July

A little-known story in the Bible is that of Bezalel, who was called upon by God to design and build the Tabernacle, a sacred place of worship for the Israelites during their journey through the desert. Bezalel was a craftsman, endowed with great talent and the wisdom to accomplish this task.

It reminds you that I have also gifted you with specific talents and skills. These are not just the obvious or widely recognised ones, but also the more discreet gifts, the ones that can go unnoticed. Every talent, every skill, every passion you have is a blessing I have placed in you. Use them wisely, with love and generosity, to make the world a better and brighter place. You are important and your work is of great value to me.

# 16 July

Remember the story of Elisha, who received a double portion of Elijah's spirit when he was taken up in a whirlwind. Elisha went on to perform many miracles in my name, despite the challenges and opposition he encountered. It's not always easy to face up to life, and you may feel overwhelmed by the difficulties and obstacles. But know that I'm with you through every trial. I give you the strength to carry on, even when you feel weak. I support you, even when you feel like you're buckling under the weight of your problems.

With me by your side, you can overcome every challenge that comes your way. So keep hoping, be courageous and continue to show faith. Your resilience is a light to those around you, a testament to my love and grace working in you.

# 17 July

Remember the story of Gideon, the man I chose to free Israel from the Midianites. Even though Gideon saw himself as the least of his family, I saw in him a valiant warrior. It's not unusual for you to feel small, insignificant or incapable. But I assure you that you are invaluable to me. I see you not as you are now, but as you can become. I see in you enormous potential, talents and abilities just waiting to be developed. Don't be afraid to do the things you think are impossible. With me, nothing is out of reach. I'll help you grow, develop and achieve everything you set your heart on. Share your fears, uncertainties and doubts with me, and let me guide you along the path that leads to the fulfilment of your aspirations.

# 18th July

I am the First and the Last, the Living One; I was dead, and behold, I am alive for ever and ever. I am the Alpha and the Omega, the beginning and the end, the first and the last. It is I who give you strength when the world around you seems to be falling apart. As described in the Apocalypse, there will be times when the world seems to be full of turmoil. It is during these times that I want you to remember My promise - the promise of the new Jerusalem, the holy city, coming down from heaven, adorned like a bride adorned for her husband. There will be no more tears, no more death, no more crying, no more pain. So don't let yourself be overwhelmed by the trials of this life. Your future is assured in the city of God, where the light of God and the Lamb illuminates all things. Remain strong in your faith and seek Me in everything you do. Know that I am with you, even to the end of time.

# 19 July

Today, let me tell you about Queen Esther. Esther was a young Jewish girl in the Persian Empire who became queen through a fortunate set of circumstances. When a plan was hatched to exterminate all the Jews in the empire, Esther risked her life to save her people.

Esther showed incredible faith and courage in the face of terrifying circumstances. She wasn't sure what would happen, but she trusted God and did what she thought was right.

Today I ask you to show the same courage in your own life. Face your fears, stand up for what's right, even if it's difficult. And remember that I am always by your side to support and guide you.

# 20th July

I invite you to remember the message of the Apocalypse, a book of hope despite its terrifying images. In difficult times, when life seems as chaotic and unpredictable as the visions of John of Patmos, don't forget that every story, every life, has a promising ending. Like the new Eden that emerges from the ruins of the Apocalypse, I assure you that a new creation awaits every person who persists in faith and love.

Remember that victory has already been won, that love has triumphed over death. And as in the Apocalypse, every difficulty, every tribulation, is an opportunity for transformation and rebirth. Do not fear trials, for it is through them that you become stronger, wiser and closer to me. So courage, my dear. As John of Patmos wrote, "He who perseveres to the end will be saved". Persevere in faith, and you will see the new Eden that awaits you.

# 21 July

Today I want to talk to you about the inexhaustible love of the Father. In Genesis, when the first human couple fell, God did not abandon His creation. He put in place a plan of salvation, proving that nothing can separate His creation from His love. That same love is available to you today. No matter what mistakes you've made or how many times you've fallen, the Father is waiting for you with open arms, ready to forgive you and restore you.

Rest assured that nothing can separate you from God's love. Neither failures, nor disappointments, nor even the worst mistakes can put an end to that love. So don't hesitate to come back to Him, because He is always waiting for you with the same unconditional love.

## 22 July

Today, remember the love I have for you. A love that transcends time and space, a love that is unconditional and infinite. You are precious to me, one of a kind, and I shed my blood for you on the Cross.

In your everyday life, allow this love to influence you, to guide your words and your actions. Let every interaction be an opportunity to spread this love around you, to reflect the light I have placed within you. May you see beyond the challenges of the present moment and realise how much you are loved, not only by those around you, but also and above all by Me. I am always with you, in every breath, in every beat of your heart. May you find comfort and strength in this unshakeable love. Amen.

## 23 July

On this day, I remind you never to forget the importance of faith. Faith is that little flame in your heart that keeps you going even when times are hard. It's the anchor that keeps you steady in the storms of life. Faith doesn't require you to understand everything, just to trust. In the book of Matthew, I said, "If you had faith like a mustard seed, you would say to this mountain, 'Move from here to there,' and it would move; nothing would be impossible for you." (Matthew 17:20). This power of faith is within you. It can enable you to accomplish incredible things and overcome seemingly insurmountable obstacles.

So, today and every day, I encourage you to keep the faith. Even when things seem dark, even when you feel lost, keep the faith. For it is faith that will guide you into the light. Amen.

## 24 July

Today, I want you to reflect on the passage in the Bible where I fed the five thousand people with just five loaves and two fish (Matthew 14:13-21). It was a time when resources seemed inadequate, but yet, with faith, the impossible became possible.

In your own life, you may sometimes feel limited or overwhelmed by your problems. Maybe you feel like those disciples, looking at the five loaves and two fish, wondering how they could be enough. But remember this story and know that no matter how limited or overwhelmed you feel, with faith you can do much more than you think you're capable of.

So this day, don't let your doubts or fears limit you. Instead, remember the multiplication of the loaves and fishes, and know that I am at work with you, in the big and small moments of your life. Entrust your fears and doubts to me, and see how I can transform them into something beautiful and abundant. Amen.

## 25 July

Think of the story of Martha and Mary (Luke 10:38-42). Martha, absorbed in her tasks, couldn't understand why Mary preferred to sit and listen to my words. So I said to her, "Mary has chosen the better part."

Like Martha, you may feel overwhelmed by life's obligations. But I invite you to remember Mary. To take the time to stop, to listen to me, to rest. This moment of quiet is a precious gift that will always be offered to you. Amen.

## 26 July

Remember the Sea of Galilee, where, with a simple "Silence!" I calmed the storm (Mark 4:39). In your life too, there may be storms, challenges and fears. But don't forget, I'm with you always. No storm is too great for me, no challenge insurmountable. I am the master of the wind and the waves. I can calm raging seas and soothe troubled hearts. As I did for my disciples in the boat that day on the Sea of Galilee, I am there for you. There, in your fear and uncertainty. I am peace in the storm. On this day, I invite you to trust me, even in the midst of life's raging waves. When everything around you seems unstable, know that I am stable. I am your rock, your safe refuge. Do not be afraid, for I am with you. Look not to the storm, but to me.

I say to you today: "Don't be afraid". With me, you can get through any trial. Keep your eyes fixed on me, and not on the waves. For I am the Prince of Peace, and I offer you a peace that passes all understanding. Amen.

## 27 July

Remember the time when I washed the feet of my disciples, a demonstration of humility and love. As I have loved you, I invite you to love others, to serve without expecting anything in return.

True love is patient and kind. It is not jealous, it is not boastful, it is not proud. When you love as I have loved you, you share in the work I have begun.

So today, look for opportunities to serve, to give and to love. Don't let resistance or indifference discourage you, because every act of love counts. Amen.

## 28 July

Remember the story of the woman at the well. She came to fetch water, but found much more than that. She found truth, love and acceptance, even if her life wasn't perfect.

As I did for her, I also want to show you that no matter where you are in life, no matter your past or your mistakes, my love for you is unconditional. There's always hope and a place for you at my table.

So don't hide in shame or regret. Approach with confidence and know that you are loved, that you are valuable and that you have a purpose. Amen.

## 29th July

Have you ever heard of the parable of the barren fig tree? I told of a caretaker who asked for more time to cultivate and fertilise his fig tree, in the hope that it would eventually bear fruit.

It represents you. No matter how many times you've stumbled or failed to bear fruit, I won't abandon you. I'm here to nourish you, to help you grow. I believe in you, in your potential to bear fruit of love, joy, peace and kindness.

Never lose hope in yourself, because I never lose hope in you. Keep trying, keep growing and become the best version of yourself. Amen to that.

# 30th July

Do you remember the story of the widow of Zarephath in the first book of Kings? A poor woman without much hope, who despite her desperate situation showed immense generosity towards the prophet Elijah. She shared her last morsel of bread with him, and in return I miraculously multiplied her oil and flour, so that she never lacked for food.

In your life, you may find yourself in situations that seem hopeless. You may feel that you have nothing left to give. Yet, like the widow of Sarepta, when you share generously, even in adversity, you open the way to my miraculous grace.

I encourage you to have the faith of this widow. Despite your circumstances, trust in my love and my provision. Even in the darkest moments, my light can shine and transform your situation. Amen.


# 31 July

When you wander, I'm there for you, your shelter and your refreshment. Your daily life - family, work, love - are wellsprings of joy and comfort. Cultivate these moments with care.

Remember, true satisfaction comes from the living water I provide. The pleasures of the world may quench your thirst, but my water will refresh your soul forever.

Stay close to me, and I will continue to offer you this living water. May your life be a fountain of my love, overflowing onto those around you. Amen.

## 1st August

A new day is dawning, an invitation to live and love, to work and enjoy. Every day is a new page in your story with me.

Look around you, do you see the beauty of creation, the rhythm of life, the movement of love? All this is for you, for your happiness and fulfilment. Take the time to stop, look, listen and feel. My love is everywhere, in the laughter of a child, in the support of a friend, in the daily toil that bears fruit. Look for me in the little things, because that's where I often reveal myself.

May this day be a blessing for you and those you meet. Amen.


## 2 August


As dawn breaks, I invite you to a new day, filled with new possibilities and graces to receive. Remember that every interaction, every task, every moment can become a sanctuary, a place of encounter with Me.

In the quiet of your home, in the hustle and bustle of work, in the sharing with loved ones, I'm there with you. I see you, I know you, I love you. The simplicity of everyday life can become fertile ground for your spiritual growth, if you invite me.

May this day bring you even closer to Me, through every smile shared, every hand extended, every word of love spoken. May you be a source of joy and peace for everyone you meet.

On this new day, I bless you and I'm with you.

## 3 August

As this new day dawns, I invite you to look deep inside yourself, to discover the richness that lies within you, the light that beckons you to shine. You have immense inner strength, infinite potential waiting to be revealed. I'm here to guide you on this inner journey.

Remember that every failure, every obstacle, is an opportunity to grow, to learn and to draw closer to Me. Resilience is a precious gift that I have given you. Use it to overcome life's challenges and to move forward with courage and determination.

Be silent within yourself and listen to the gentle, persistent voice guiding you towards the realisation of your true self. You are unique, you are precious, you are loved. Don't let anyone extinguish your light. I'm here to help you make it shine.

May your day be rich in discoveries and learning. May your inner strength guide you towards the fulfilment of your dreams. I am with you, today and always. I am with you, today and always. Amen.

## 4 August

Remember today, you are a constantly evolving work of art. Every strength and weakness, every victory and failure, shape your unique life. Accept yourself, for you are the image of My love.

Be bold, be courageous. Failure is an opportunity for growth, success an opportunity for humility. I'm with you every step of the way, your love for you is unconditional and eternal.

Remember, you are precious and capable of great things. Amen.

## 5 August

Never forget that life is a journey, not a destination. Every moment, every breath, is an opportunity to learn and grow. Don't worry about what you don't know yet, because every day brings new opportunities to learn.

Be gentle with yourself. Don't punish yourself for past mistakes, but learn from them. Accept your imperfections, for it is through them that My grace shines. Keep fighting, keep hoping, keep dreaming.

I'm with you every step of the way. My love surrounds you and sustains you. My love surrounds you and sustains you. Amen.

## 6 August

Always remember that the greatest power lies in love. Love yourself, love others, love the life you've been given. Never let life's challenges make you bitter or cynical, but turn every trial into an opportunity to love more.

Gentleness and compassion are signs of strength, not weakness. Never be afraid to be kind, even when the world may seem harsh and insensitive. Know that I am with you, guiding and supporting you through the difficulties.

In loneliness, I am your company. In sadness, I am your comfort. In happiness, I share your joy. You are never alone, for I am always at your side. Amen.

# 7 August

Don't underestimate the value of each day I give you. Every moment is a blessing, an opportunity to grow, learn and love. Every experience is a valuable lesson, sculpting your soul and shaping your character. Life's challenges are not there to break you, but to strengthen you. They are tools for your growth, means to help you discover who you really are. Even in times of pain and confusion, know that I am there, offering you my peace and comfort.

In every circumstance, seek to see the light of my love. Even in the darkest moments, know that my presence is by your side, guiding you towards peace and happiness. Amen.

# 8 August

Remember, every morning is a new beginning, a chance to redirect your heart and mind towards what really matters. Choose gratitude and optimism as your companions. Let each of life's experiences teach and transform you, bringing you closer to truth and wisdom.

The mistakes you made yesterday don't define who you are today. They are steps on the ladder of your growth, showing you where you need to learn and change. With each new day, I offer you the chance to start again, to rise above your failures and take another step towards fulfilling your destiny.

May your day be filled with joy, love and peace. May every moment be an opportunity to appreciate the wonders that surround you. Amen.

# 9 August

In those moments when you may feel abandoned, know that I am always there with you. Even though life's challenges can sometimes seem overwhelming, remember that every experience, however difficult, is part of a greater plan.

When the world seems to be collapsing around you, have the strength to turn to me. I am the constant in this ever-changing universe. Let me help you turn your feelings of abandonment into greater strength.

Entrust yourself to me, knowing that even when you feel abandoned, I'm here to guide and protect you. I am your refuge and your strength. I am your refuge and your strength. Amen.

# 10 August

In life, failure is inevitable, but know that even in your failures, I'm there with you. Don't see failure as an end, but as an opportunity to learn and grow.

Every failure is a lesson, a chance to grow and become stronger. Although the disappointment can be overwhelming, remember that I'm here to help you get back on your feet and move on.

Failure is not a sign of weakness, but a sign of courage. It's proof that you tried, that you took risks and that you weren't afraid to move forward. Be brave, be strong and know that I am always with you. Amen.

## 11 August

Health is a precious gift, and it's often in times of illness or weakness that we realise its value. I see you, and I understand your pain and worries. I'm with you, supporting you, offering you comfort.

Remember that even in pain and suffering, there are lessons to be learned and strength to be gained. Illness may seem like an insurmountable ordeal to you, but remember that I'm by your side, ready to offer you my help and my healing.

Trust me in these moments, and let me guide you towards healing. Remember that your health is measured not just by the absence of disease, but also by a feeling of peace and well-being. I'm here to give you that. Amen.

## 12 August

In this world, there are moments of failure, moments when despite your best efforts, things don't go according to plan. These moments can seem dark and discouraging, but I'm here with you.

Remember that failure is not the end, it's simply a step on the road to success. It offers valuable lessons and gives you the opportunity to grow and strengthen yourself. Don't let failure get you down, but use it as an opportunity to learn and move forward.

With each failure, you become stronger, wiser and more resilient. Failure is not an indication of your worth, but an indicator of your progress. I am with you in these moments, supporting you and guiding you to future success. Amen to that.

# 13 August

In moments of calm, when the day is drawing to a close and the stars begin to twinkle in the sky, I suggest that you seek peace. Let this peace be not simply an absence of conflict, but an active presence of serenity and tranquillity in your heart.

Let the worries and tensions of the day dissolve in acceptance of what is. Let each breath bring you more peace, more calm. Know that I'm here, that I'm the peace you're looking for.

But remember too that peace is an active quest, requiring courage and resilience. Peace is not always easy to achieve, but it is worth the effort. Peace is a gift you give yourself, a gift I encourage you to cherish.

In peace, you will find clarity, love and compassion. In peace, you will find the strength to carry on, even in difficult times. And in peace, you will always find me by your side, supporting and guiding you. Amen.

# 14 August

Remember today, in your quest for personal development, that you are not alone. I'm here to help you find the courage within yourself. Faced with the unknown, it's normal to be afraid, but know that you can transform these feelings into curiosity and courage.

Every challenge you face is a chance to grow. Every failure an opportunity to learn. And every success, big or small, is worth celebrating. I'm with you through it all, supporting you every step of the way.

# 15 August

Today I invite you to meditate on the often neglected figures of the Bible, the minorities who played such an important role in salvation history. Think of the Queen of Sheba, who came from afar to seek Solomon's wisdom, or the foreigner Ruth, whose loyalty to her mother-in-law led to the birth of David.

Remember, on this day, that everyone has a place in the Kingdom of God, whatever their origin or condition. Everyone is precious in My eyes, and every story, no matter how small, is an important part of the great story of God's love.

# 16 August

I, Jesus, guide you today to contemplate the wonder of creation. Consider the story of Noah, a righteous man who was chosen to save a piece of every living thing on Earth. In this act, see the importance that God gives to all life, to every organism, large or small.

Creation is a gift, a sign of God's infinite love for us. Today, take a moment to appreciate the beauty and complexity of the world around you. See in every creature, in every plant, in every rock, a reflection of God's love.

# 17 August

Remember, dear ones, the story of Ruth in the Scriptures. A woman who, despite loss and strangeness, chose loyalty and love. Her devotion to her mother-in-law Naomi, her willingness to work hard and her choice to embrace an unknown faith are testament to her strength of character and resilience.

Like Ruth, you too may find yourself facing moments of great loss and radical change. But know that in these moments, God's grace is present. Have the courage to embrace change, to love deeply and to choose faithfulness. It is in these moments that we can truly discover who we are and what we are called to become.


# 18 August

Think about the importance of work and rest in the Bible. When God created the world, He worked for six days and then rested on the seventh. This was not because He was tired, but to establish a rhythm of work and rest that we should follow. The Bible also teaches us the value and dignity of work. In the book of Proverbs, laziness is reproved while diligent work is praised. Paul, in his epistles, exhorts us to work with our own hands to provide for ourselves and others.

But don't forget that your true vocation is to love and serve God and your neighbour. Let your work be a way of living out this vocation. And don't forget to rest, to take time to recharge your batteries, to pray and to draw closer to God. Know that I am with you in your moments of work and in your moments of rest.

## 19 August

On this day, I invite you to reflect on these words from the Gospel according to Matthew: "If your brother has sinned, go and rebuke him between you and him alone. If he listens to you, you have gained your brother." (Matthew 18:15). Understanding this lesson means realising that conflicts, even though they can be difficult and painful, are an opportunity to grow and become closer to the other person. Dialogue, listening and sincerity are the keys to overcoming obstacles and finding harmony.

May you today, and every day, approach conflict not with anger or rancour, but with a heart open to understanding and reconciliation. Then you will be able to say, like the apostle Paul: "We strive to live at peace with everyone and to live holy lives; for without this, no one will see the Lord" (Hebrews 12:14).

## 20 August

Today, I invite you to reflect on another dimension of conflict resolution: forgiveness. In the epistle to the Colossians, it is written: "Bear with one another, and if one has a complaint against another, forgive one another; as the Lord has forgiven you, so do you" (Colossians 3:13). Forgiveness is not a sign of weakness, but rather of strength. It does not erase the wound, but opens the way to healing. It does not deny the pain of the past, but allows us to free ourselves from its weight.

May this day be an opportunity for you to practise forgiveness, to free your hearts of resentment and to open yourselves to the possibility of reconciliation. May you say with sincerity: "As the Lord has forgiven us, so we forgive those who trespass against us".

## 21 August

Let's reflect today on the place of work in our lives, from a biblical perspective. Scripture tells us: "All work deserves its reward" (1 Timothy 5:18). These words remind us of the value of work and the importance of being rewarded for our efforts.

Let's not forget that work is not simply a means of subsistence, but also a way of participating in God's work of creation. Every task performed with love and dedication is a reflection of our creativity and humanity.

Today, may you find pleasure and meaning in your work, may you be appreciated for your efforts, and may you participate in the work of divine creation through the labour of your hands.

## 22 August

The Bible also has lessons to teach us about rest. In the book of Exodus, God commands: "Six days you shall labour, but on the seventh day you shall rest; even in the time of ploughing and reaping you shall rest" (Exodus 34:21).

This verse reminds us of the importance of rest, not only for our physical well-being, but also for our spiritual well-being. Rest is not an escape from work, but a sacred time to recharge our strength, renew our spirit and thank God for the fruits of our labour.

On this day, may you find rest in God's presence, be restored by His love and be filled with gratitude for the gift of work and rest.

# 23 August

Today we explore the issue of conflict and how the Bible guides us in dealing with it. In his letter to the Ephesians, the apostle Paul writes: "Do not let the sun go down on your anger" (Ephesians 4:26). These words invite us to resolve our conflicts quickly and respectfully, so that resentment does not take root in our hearts.

Conflict, if well managed, can become an opportunity to grow, to understand the other person and to strengthen our bonds. The key is to deal with it with love, respect and humility, always seeking to understand the other person's point of view.

May you have the wisdom and courage to resolve conflicts in a spirit of love and respect. May the peace of God reign in your hearts and in your relationships.

# 24 August

Let's not forget that the Bible, while providing advice on how to deal with conflict, also stresses the importance of forgiveness. In the Gospel of Matthew, we are told: "If your brother has sinned, rebuke him; if he repents, forgive him" (Matthew 18:15).

Forgiveness, although sometimes difficult to give, is a liberating act that frees us from resentment and spite. It is also a demonstration of our love for others, despite their mistakes.

Today, may you have the courage to forgive those who have offended you, may you find freedom in forgiveness, and may you love unconditionally, as God loves you.

# 25 August

Our journey through the biblical themes leads us today to the idea of providence and trust in God. In the book of Jeremiah we read: "For I know the plans I have for you, says the Lord, plans for peace and not for evil, to give you a future and a hope" (Jeremiah 29:11). This verse reminds us that even in the most difficult times, we must maintain our trust in God, knowing that he has a plan for us. It invites us to remain hopeful and to believe in God's providence, even when things don't seem to be going our way. On this day, may your trust in God be strengthened. May you find peace and hope in his providence, and may you know that even in the darkest of times, God has a plan for you.

# 26 August

Today we look at the story of Joseph, who was sold by his brothers out of jealousy, but who eventually rose to a position of great power in Egypt. In Genesis, Joseph says to his brothers: "You planned to do me harm, but God has turned it to good, to accomplish what is happening today: the life of a numerous people is saved" (Genesis 50:20). This passage reminds us that even in the most difficult times, there is a possibility of good. Joseph was betrayed by his own brothers, but he showed resilience and was able to save many lives during a famine. May this day inspire us to have faith even in difficult times, to be resilient in the face of adversity and to always look for the good in every situation. May we, like Joseph, show forgiveness and understanding to those who have hurt us.

## 27 August

In the book of Daniel, we meet Shadrach, Meshach and Abednego, three young men who chose to remain faithful to God even in the face of the possibility of being thrown into a fiery furnace. Their courage and faith were rewarded when God saved them from that fiery ordeal. May that same courage and faith dwell in you, so that you may always remain faithful to what is right, even in the face of adversity. Remember that every trial is an opportunity to show your resilience and dedication to your faith. Like these three men, remain steadfast, for I am with you through every trial.

## 28 August

In the Acts of the Apostles, we see the example of the apostle Paul who, despite many trials and persecutions, continued to preach the Gospel with boldness. Once a persecutor of Christians, he became one of the greatest apostles of the Gospel. May this story encourage you to believe in the possibility of transformation and change, whatever your past. You are capable of growing and transforming yourself, just as Paul did. Your past does not define your future, but rather the choices you make today. May your faith in Me inspire you to live a life of love, generosity and forgiveness.

## 29 August

In the book of Exodus, we see how Moses was called by God to lead the people of Israel out of Egypt, to freedom. Despite his fear and doubts, Moses answered the call. This story shows us that even if we are afraid, even if we doubt ourselves, God can use us to achieve great things. Every day, I call you to live by my commandments and to be an instrument of my love. May you find the strength to respond to this call, even when you are afraid, and may you trust in My presence that accompanies you every step of the way.

## 30 August

In the book of Jeremiah, Jeremiah himself is an example of endurance and unshakeable faith despite persecution and rejection. Despite the many difficulties he encountered, Jeremiah remained faithful to his mission as a prophet and continued to deliver God's messages to his people. May his example remind you of the importance of remaining faithful to your convictions and your faith, even if that means facing challenges and difficulties. Know that I am with you in these moments and that My grace is sufficient for you.

# 31 August

Don't forget the story of Gideon, a judge of Israel who, despite his doubts and feelings of insignificance, led his people to a surprising victory with just 300 men. This is proof that I can use anyone, no matter how you see yourself or how others see you. May the story of Gideon remind you that you are precious in My eyes and that you are capable of doing incredible things by My grace. Continue to believe in yourself and in My presence within you. Like Gideon, may you find the courage and confidence to answer My call. Trust that I will provide you with everything you need to accomplish the mission I have given you.

# 1st September

Remember the faith of the Canaanite woman who, despite initial rejection, insisted on obtaining healing for her daughter. She demonstrated a bold and persistent faith that was rewarded. May this story inspire you to show similar faith in your life, especially when things seem difficult. Never abandon your faith, for it is through it that you can receive My blessings. I'm always here for you, ready to listen and answer your prayers. Like the Canaanite woman, may you persevere in your faith, even in the face of adversity. I am with you, always ready to extend My grace and My love.

# 2 September

Remember the lesson of the parable of the sower. The same message can fall on different soil, and depending on the soil, it can prosper or die out. The Word is sown generously, but its reception depends on the state of the heart of the listener. Let your heart today be fertile soil, welcoming My words with joy, and allowing them to take root and bear much fruit. Be resistant to the distractions, temptations and trials of life that might try to stifle the Word in you. Let My Word resonate within you, guiding and strengthening you, so that you can bear good fruit in your life.

# 3 September

Think of the story of Joshua, who succeeded Moses as leader of the Israelites. Despite challenges and adversity, he remained strong and courageous, guided by his unshakeable faith in Me. He led the Israelites across the Jordan and took possession of the promised land. May you, like Joshua, show courage and determination in the face of life's challenges. Remember that I am with you always, just as I was with Joshua. May you have the strength and courage to go forward, knowing that you are never alone and that I am always there to guide you.

# 4 September

Consider the path of Abigail, a woman of good sense and good looks who showed wisdom in appeasing the anger of the future king David. She acted swiftly, with grace and wisdom, and avoided unnecessary bloodshed. May her wisdom guide you in your actions, and may you also show such discernment and diplomacy in your interactions with others. May you remember that a gentle word can turn away anger, and that well-placed wisdom can bring peace where chaos reigns. May his courage in the face of adversity inspire and guide you along the path of good.

# 5 September

Meditate on the story of Ananias, a disciple in Damascus, who obeyed My instruction to visit Saul of Tarsus, despite his fear. He put his trust in Me, enabling Saul to become Paul, an essential apostle in spreading My word. May you also, in the face of fear, place your trust in Me, knowing that My plan is greater than what you can see or understand. May you feel My love and support when you face seemingly insurmountable challenges, knowing that I am always with you, guiding your steps along the path of justice and truth.

# 6 September

Get up every day knowing that every moment is a blessing, an opportunity to grow and flourish. Let every task, however insignificant, be an opportunity to express your love and devotion. May every interaction, no matter how trivial, be a moment of connection, of sharing My light with others. Each of your actions, however small, has an importance in the great plan of the universe. May your daily life be a living prayer, a tribute to the love and grace that I have poured into you.

# 7 September

Every day brings its share of challenges and joys. In the routine of everyday life, it's easy to lose sight of the beauty and miracle of life. Remember, every moment is precious and deserves to be lived to the full. May you find comfort in simplicity, joy in the little things and peace in every quiet moment. Remember that I am present in every gesture of love, in every smile shared, in every word of kindness. Every day is a chance to show those around you how much they are loved and precious. May you see My presence in every aspect of your daily life.

# 8 September

My love for you is present in every breath you take. May your thoughts, actions and words be filled with kindness and compassion. When you feel overwhelmed by the difficulties of everyday life, remember that you are not alone. I am by your side, supporting and guiding you through every trial. May you always find courage and strength in My constant presence. Take the time to appreciate the little moments of joy and serenity that dot your path, for they are what make life precious. Be open to receiving My love, and let it guide your steps.

# 9 September

Every day is a new opportunity to love, learn and grow. Whatever tasks await you, treat them all with diligence and love. May the joy of a job well done fill you with deep satisfaction. May you see the good side of things, even in the most difficult moments. For every challenge is an opportunity for growth, and every difficulty is a chance to become stronger. May you find beauty in every moment and grace in everything. Every act of love and kindness you perform sows seeds of goodness that will blossom to beautify the world around you.

# 10 September

Every morning is a new promise, every sunrise a blessing. Don't let yourself be overwhelmed by the cares of the world, but welcome each day with a spirit of gratitude. Seek to discover beauty in the simple things of life, and to appreciate moments of peace and tranquillity. May every encounter bring you closer to your neighbour, and may every act of kindness light your way a little more. May you always remember that you are surrounded by My love and that you are never alone, even in moments of doubt and uncertainty. Be the reflection of My love in the world.

# 11 September

Today, take the time to rest and recharge your batteries. Remember that rest is as important as work in maintaining the balance of your being. Take the time to meditate, to pray, to reconnect with Me. In the silence of your heart, you will find the peace and serenity you need to face the challenges of everyday life. Remember that I am always there, offering you My strength and support. May you feel My presence in every breath you take, in every beat of your heart. Be assured of My unconditional love for you.

# 12 September

Every act of love you show, every kind gesture you make, resonates in the world like a musical note, adding to the universal harmony. Know that even the smallest gestures have an impact, and that you have the power to make a difference in someone's life, even in the most subtle ways. Take a moment today to look around you, to recognise the beauty and goodness that exists in the world. Allow this love to guide and strengthen you in your daily actions. You are precious in My eyes, and I am with you every moment.

# 13 September

Sometimes life can seem like a complex labyrinth, but don't forget that I'm always with you to guide you. Take time to listen to My voice in the silence of your heart, gently guiding you along the path of peace and joy. Don't be discouraged by difficulties, for they are often opportunities to grow and learn. May trust in My presence give you the courage and determination you need to overcome the challenges of your daily life. You are loved, cherished and never alone in your trials.

## 14 September

Forgiveness is a powerful force, a gift of love that you can offer to yourself and to others. It's not about forgetting or minimising pain, but about letting go of the resentment and anger that poison your heart. By forgiving, you free yourself from these burdens and open the door to healing and reconciliation. Remember that I am always ready to forgive, and I invite you to do the same. Let love and compassion replace anger and resentment. It's a journey that requires courage and patience, but know that I'm with you every step of the way. Let your heart be open to forgiveness, so that you can live in the freedom of My love.

## 15 September

Money is a tool that can be used for good or for evil. It is neither good nor bad in itself, but depends on how you use it. Don't be blinded by greed, but use your resources wisely and generously. Don't forget the less fortunate and show compassion towards those who have less. Money can bring comfort, but true wealth is found in the love, compassion and kindness you share with others. Seek first the kingdom of heaven, and everything else will be given to you in addition. And know that the real treasure is not counted in gold coins, but in acts of love and kindness.

# 16 September

Patience is a virtue that brings peace and tranquillity in times of turmoil. When you're feeling frustrated or anxious, remember that every situation has an end, and that patience can help you get through these moments more calmly. Learn to wait, not to rush, and to accept that some things take time. Be patient with yourself and with others, because everyone moves at their own pace. And don't forget that I am with you, in the moments of waiting as in those of action. My patience is infinite, and I ask you to have the same patience with yourself and with others.

# 17 September

Joy is not a question of circumstances, but of attitude. Even in the darkest moments, you can find reasons to rejoice. Look for the beauty in the little things, the gestures of love, the smiles, the birdsong, the sunset... Joy is a gift that you can choose to receive every day. Don't wait for circumstances to change before you rejoice, but choose joy, even in the midst of difficulties. And don't forget that I am with you, bringing joy to your heart, whatever the circumstances. Take pleasure in every moment and let My joy fill your heart.

# 18 September

Every day is a new opportunity to learn and grow. Don't be afraid of failure, because it's often the prelude to success. Mistakes are not a sign of weakness, but an indication that you need to learn something new. Approach every challenge with the attitude of a learner, ready to learn from every experience. Whether you succeed or fail, I'm with you, guiding and encouraging you to keep learning and growing. Know that every challenge is an opportunity in disguise, a chance to deepen your resilience and wisdom. As you look to the future, don't forget that I'm by your side, giving you strength and courage.

# 19 September

Don't forget the importance of gratitude. It's easy to focus on what's going wrong in life, but it's just as important to recognise the blessings and moments of joy. Gratitude can turn an ordinary day into a day of celebration. It can brighten dark moments and bring peace in the midst of chaos. Take time each day to give thanks for the blessings, big and small, you've received. And remember that every good thing comes from Me, because I love you and I want you to be happy. When you express your gratitude, you invite joy into your heart and create space for even more blessings. It's a virtuous circle that enriches your spirit and your soul.

# 20 September

Patience is a precious virtue. It teaches you to wait, to have hope even when the results you want are not immediate. Patience helps you to understand that God's time is not your time, that His plan is perfect even if it doesn't work out the way you want. Never forget that I have promised to give you what you need at the right time. Patience invites you to trust in My love for you, to know that I am working for your good. So, even if the road is long, don't despair. Your patience will be rewarded with unexpected blessings.

# 21 September

It's essential to take time for yourself, to rest and recharge your batteries. Even in the hustle and bustle of daily life, I invite you to find moments of calm and tranquillity to reconnect with Me. Prayer, meditation and contemplation of nature are all ways of renewing your mind and soul. Never forget that you are not alone in your struggles. I'm here with you, ready to offer comfort and support. Find time to rest in Me, to refresh and strengthen yourself. Your body, mind and soul need these moments of rest to be at their best.

## 22 September

Health is not just the absence of disease or infirmity; it is a state of complete physical, mental and spiritual well-being. I invite you to take care of your body, because it is the temple of the Holy Spirit. Eat healthily, exercise regularly, get enough sleep and avoid harmful behaviour. Take care of your mind by nurturing positive thoughts and cultivating inner peace. Take care of your soul by clinging to My Word and keeping faith in Me. May My peace and joy accompany you in every aspect of your health. Your health is precious, do not neglect it. Always remember that I am with you, offering healing and comfort in times of need.

## 23 September

The family is a blessing that I have given to mankind. It is the place where love, respect, mutual help and patience must reign. I gave you birth to a family so that you would learn unconditional love, tolerance and sharing. Your family is a precious gift, whether it's your biological family or the one you've chosen. Love them, respect them, support them and forgive them, because they are your first contact with the world and with love. I am the Father of all, and you are all brothers and sisters in My great family. Cherish these moments with your family, for they are sacred. And remember, family is not just a bond of blood, it's above all a bond of love and respect.

# 24 September

Friends are a blessing that I have placed in your life to bring you joy, support and love. They are there to share your joys, ease your sorrows, support you in your trials and celebrate your victories. A true friend loves at all times and becomes a brother in adversity. Treat your friends with respect, love and loyalty, as you would like to be treated. Remember that, like you, they are My children and worthy of your love and respect. Love them, respect them and support them, for a true friend is a precious rarity. But also remember that I am your most faithful friend, the One who will never abandon you.

# 25 September

Betrayal is a painful and difficult ordeal to go through. When you feel betrayed, remember My own experience of betrayal, when I was betrayed by one of My own. I understand your pain and I am there to console you. Betrayal can cause a lot of pain, but it can also make you grow in strength and wisdom. Forgive those who have betrayed you, not because they deserve it, but because you deserve peace. Remember that I am here to help you heal and find peace. Forgive, as I have forgiven you, for forgiveness frees your heart from pain and allows you to move forward with love and wisdom.

## 26 September

Generosity is a virtue that I encourage in you. Don't be afraid to give generously, whether of your time, your talents or your resources. As the Word says, he who gives generously receives in return. Be generous not to receive, but because it is a reflection of My love in you. Share freely what you have, as I freely share My blessings with you. And remember, there is no small gift. Every gesture counts. Every smile, every word of encouragement, every act of compassion, they are all precious in My eyes. For true generosity lies in the love you put into each of your gestures.

## 27 September

Doubt can sometimes invade your mind and heart, causing confusion and uncertainty. Know that even in these moments, I am with you. Doubt is not a sign of weakness, but an opportunity to deepen your faith. When you doubt, seek Me and I will give you the wisdom and guidance you need. Don't forget that I am the truth, and in Me are all the answers. Keep your faith in Me, even in the midst of doubts, and I will enlighten you. May these moments of doubt bring you closer to Me, allowing you to question yourself, to explore your faith and to deepen your love for Me. Know that in doubt, you are growing, and through this growth, you are drawing closer to Me.

# 28 September

In the quest for truth, it's natural to ask questions, to have doubts, to seek and explore. Remember that I am the truth. In your exploration, seek Me. Seek to know Me more intimately, for that is how you will find the truth you seek. Let your search for truth be not just an intellectual endeavour, but also a spiritual one. Seek not only facts, but also wisdom and spiritual understanding. For the truth you seek is found in Me, and in seeking Me you will find it.

# 29 September

Loneliness can sometimes make you feel like you're all alone in the world, forgotten and neglected. But remember, you're never really alone. I am always with you. You are precious to Me and you mean a lot to Me. Don't let the feeling of loneliness fool you. Instead, use these moments to draw closer to Me. Spend time in My presence, praying and meditating. Let Me console and reassure you. For even in the midst of loneliness, My love for you remains constant and unshakeable.

# September 30th

Life can sometimes seem like a complex labyrinth, with many paths to take, unexpected turns and dead ends. In these moments, remember that I am the ultimate guide. Come to Me when you feel lost or confused. Ask Me for the direction and clarity you seek. There may be times when the path I guide you to take may not seem to make sense, but know that My plan for you is always for your good. Trust Me and My guidance, and you will find your way.

# 1st October

Life can sometimes be full of conflict and disagreement. Misunderstandings may arise, harsh words may be exchanged, feelings may be hurt. But remember that I am the Prince of Peace. I can help you resolve conflicts peacefully, communicate more effectively and repair broken relationships. Don't let yourself be overwhelmed by conflict, but turn to Me for help and advice. For with Me, peace is always possible, even in the most difficult situations.

# 2 October

Dear child, failures can be devastating. They can make you doubt yourself, your skills and even your worth. But let Me remind you that failure is not an end in itself, but a springboard to greater achievements. Don't forget that even I, Jesus, have had moments of defeat and sadness. Yet these moments do not define who I am, just as your failures do not define you. Turn to Me in those moments, and I will give you the strength to keep going.

# 3 October

Money is a tool that can bring comfort and security, but it can also cause stress and anxiety. It is important to remember that, although money can buy material goods, it cannot buy happiness, peace or love. These things can only be found in a relationship with Me. Don't be blinded by the pursuit of material wealth, but seek first the Kingdom of God and his righteousness, and all these things will be given to you in addition.

# 4 October

Loneliness can weigh heavily on your heart, my child. It's natural to long for companionship and companionship, but it's also crucial to understand that you are never truly alone. I am always by your side, even in your darkest moments. Turn to Me, and you'll find comfort. Never forget that every person you meet is an opportunity to see My love at work. Every interaction is a chance to share and receive love. Loneliness is temporary, while My love is eternal. Find comfort in Me, and you will find comfort in yourself.

# 5 October

Beloved child, I know that temptation is an inevitable part of human life. However, do not let these challenges keep you from truth and goodness. Remember that you have the strength to resist any temptation if you turn to Me for help. I am there to guide and support you, and even when you fall, I am there to lift you up. Do not fear failure, for it is a springboard to growth and wisdom. My grace is sufficient for you, for My strength is made perfect in your weakness. Trust in My love for you, even in the midst of temptation.

# 6 October

My child, gratitude is a key that opens the door to a life of fulfilment. Every day is a gift filled with blessings, large and small. I invite you to take a moment to give thanks for these blessings. Gratitude can transform an ordinary day into a celebration of joy and love. No matter what challenges you face, an attitude of gratitude can bring you profound peace. So today, and every day, I invite you to open your heart to gratitude. Remember, even in the most difficult times, there's always something to be grateful for.

# 7 October

My precious child, I see you struggling with fear. I'm here to remind you that you don't have to live in fear. Fear is a natural reaction to the unknown and the uncertain, but it doesn't have to control your life. You can lean on Me, for I am your source of strength and peace. When you face the unknown, remember My constant presence at your side. Do not be afraid, for I am with you. Do not be dismayed, for I am your God. I will strengthen you and help you; I will uphold you with My righteous right hand.

# 8 October

My child, know that forgiveness is not only a blessing you receive, but also a blessing you give. When you choose to forgive, you choose to free your heart from pain and bitterness. Forgiveness is not always easy, but it is a necessary step towards healing and freedom. Forgive as I have forgiven you. Not only will you find peace, but you will also be an instrument of My peace in the world. And when you forgive, remember that you are doing it not only for the other person, but also for yourself. By forgiving, you free yourself from the prison of resentment and open the door to a new life full of love and compassion.

# 9 October

My precious one, life may seem like a constant challenge to you, but know that every challenge is an opportunity for growth. The challenges you face are not there to break you, but to strengthen you, to forge you, to bring you to the fullness of who you are meant to be. With every difficulty, remember that I am by your side, giving you the strength and courage to overcome. Don't let your heart be troubled, and don't be afraid. Take courage, for I am with you through every trial. Every stage of your journey, every obstacle you overcome, every pain you endure, is all part of your journey of growth. Remember, My child, that even the darkest nights are followed by the dawn, and it is in these moments of challenge that you are shaped and strengthened.

# 10 October

My dear, kindness is not weakness, but a strength that shines in the darkness. It has the power to touch hearts, heal wounds and spread love. Don't be afraid to show kindness, even when the world may seem cruel and insensitive. It's at these times that your kindness is most needed. Kindness is a choice, an act of courage. By choosing to be good, you make a difference. Your kindness can light a flame in another person's heart and illuminate the world around you. Remember, my child, that the goodness you give is never lost, but spreads and brings light and love where it's needed most.

# 11 October

My child, don't forget the importance of rest. In the whirlwind of life, it's easy to get lost in the frenzy of obligations and responsibilities. But rest is essential for your well-being and personal development. Rest is not a sign of weakness, but a mark of wisdom. It gives you the opportunity to regenerate, reflect and refocus. Take the time to rest, recharge and look after yourself. Don't forget that you are precious to me and that your well-being counts. Rest is a blessing that you must give yourself so that you can give the best of yourself to others.

# 12 October

My child, know that courage is not always resounding. Sometimes there's a little voice at the end of the day that says "I'll try again tomorrow". Know that every challenge, every trial, every obstacle you encounter makes you grow, strengthens you and prepares you for the victories to come. So don't give up, even if things seem difficult. Remember that I'm always at your side to support, guide and encourage you.

# 13 October

My dear, always remember that there's no shame in asking for help. Whether you're facing a trial, feeling overwhelmed or simply need advice, don't hesitate to ask for help. We're all bound together by love and compassion, and it's in sharing our burdens that we find support, healing and the strength to carry on. Asking for help is not a sign of weakness, but an act of courage that shows your willingness to overcome difficulties. Never forget that I'm here for you, ready to offer you my unconditional help and love.

## 14 October

Dear child, I want to talk to you about gratitude. Gratitude is not only a response to a blessing received, it is also an attitude that opens your heart to receive more. Be grateful for every moment of your life - the good ones and the difficult ones - because they are all opportunities to learn, to grow and to draw closer to Me. It's in being grateful for the little things that you find true abundance. And remember, every day is a gift, every breath a blessing. So fill your heart with gratitude and let it light your way through life.

## 15 October

My child, I remind you that kindness is strength. It may seem easier to respond to hatred with hatred, but true strength lies in the ability to respond to hatred with love, to injustice with justice, and to cruelty with kindness. Never underestimate the power of a kind word, a thoughtful gesture, or even a sincere smile. These acts of kindness can transform a life, including your own. So always be generous with your kindness, for it reflects the light of My love in you. It is the divine spark that illuminates the darkness, and through it you can help heal the world.

# 16 October

My child, I understand your desire to succeed, but don't forget that it's just as important to remain humble. Success is measured not only by your achievements, but also by how you treat others and how you appreciate the little things in life. Remember, true success lies in the ability to love, give and serve. So when you reach the top, don't look down, but reach out to help others climb with you.

# 17 October

My child, remember that patience is a precious virtue. It's natural to want things to happen quickly, but sometimes the most precious things in life need time to develop. Whether it's the growth of a seed into a tree, or the development of your wisdom and compassion, patience is necessary. So don't rush, be patient and enjoy every moment of your journey. Your patience will be rewarded in due course.

# 18th October

My child, I can see that you are struggling with self-confidence issues. Know that you are my precious child and that I have created you with unique gifts and specific talents. You have within you the capacity to do great things. Believe in yourself and in what you can achieve. You are precious to me, and I am with you every step of the way. My love for you is unconditional and unending. Don't forget that you have the strength within you to overcome all the challenges you face. I encourage you to get up every day with courage and determination.

# 19 October

My child, I remind you that gratitude is an important key to a joyful and fulfilling life. Don't just look at what you lack in life, but also at all the blessings you've received. Gratitude allows you to appreciate the little moments, to find pleasure in the present and to feel truly rich. When you're feeling overwhelmed by challenges, take a moment to count your blessings. You'll be surprised to see how much you've already received. And even in difficult times, look for the hidden gifts. Remember, my grace is sufficient for you, and my power is made perfect in weakness.

# 20 October

Beloved, remember my crucifixion. It was not a moment of defeat, but rather an act of ultimate love for all of you. I took upon myself your sins, your pains, your failures and your weaknesses so that you might be freed from their weight. In difficult times, remember this sacrifice. Know that I understand your suffering, for I myself have suffered. May you find comfort and hope in this memory, and may you walk with courage and faith, knowing that I am always with you. Your pain can be transformed into strength, your grief into hope, and your despair into love, for I am with you, every step of the way.

# 21 October

My dear ones, remember my resurrection. It was the ultimate proof that life triumphs over death, love over hate, light over darkness. Through my resurrection, I want you to know that there is always hope, even in the darkest moments. No trial is too great, no problem too complex that you can't overcome with me by your side. So look to the future with confidence and hope, for you have victory in me. Resurrection is not just a story of the past, but a living reality for you today, a promise of renewal and rebirth.

# 22 October

My children, remember my trial. It symbolises the injustices of the world, but it also shows my willingness to suffer injustice out of love for you. Sometimes you may face injustice, but know that I am with you. Don't lose hope, don't be discouraged. Instead, stay strong, continue to do good and fight for justice. Even in adversity, you can be a light that shines in the darkness. My presence in your life will give you the strength to persevere, to forgive, and to transform pain into compassion and love.

# 23 October

"Knowing that the Father had given everything into my hands, and that I had come out of God and was going to God, I got up from the table, laid down my clothes and, taking a towel, girded myself. Then I poured water into a basin and began to wash the disciples' feet and to wipe them with the towel with which I was girded." (John 13:3-5)

I invite you, my beloved, to remember the humility I showed when I washed the feet of my disciples. This gesture was a teaching for you, showing you that the greatest among you must be the servant of all. May you show this humility in your daily lives, serving others with love and respect. May your spirit be imbued with this selfless love, manifesting itself in your daily actions. For in serving others, you serve me, and in so doing, you serve the Father.

# 24 October

"I am crucified with Christ; and it is no longer I who live, but Christ lives in me; what I now live in the flesh I live in faith, faith in the Son of God, who loved me and gave himself up for me." (Galatians 2:20)

As you go through life, always remember the sacrifice I made for you. I was crucified for the forgiveness of your sins and the promise of eternal life. May you live each day with renewed faith in me, recognising the immeasurable love I have for you. Only by living in me, with me and through me can you know true love. May every breath you take, every decision you make, be guided by the love and devotion you have for me, in remembrance of the sacrifice I made for you.

# 25 October

"When they had mocked me in this way, they put a purple cloak on me, saluted me and said, 'Hail, King of the Jews!' And they struck me on the head with a reed and spat on me. Then they knelt down and paid me homage." (Mark 15:17-19)

I would like to remind you how much I suffered during my trial. I endured humiliation and suffering out of love for all of you. May this inspire you to show courage in the face of life's trials. Always be prepared to endure injustice for the sake of truth. May my example help you to find the strength to endure challenges and trials with dignity and faith.

# 26 October

"On the first day of the week, Mary Magdalene went to the tomb early in the morning, while it was still dark, and saw that the stone had been removed from the tomb." (John 20:1)

I am risen, and my love for you is stronger than death. My message of eternal life is a beacon for you in times of doubt and despair. Just as Mary Magdalene discovered the empty tomb, may you also discover signs of my resurrecting presence in your daily lives. May each new day be an opportunity for you to draw closer to me, to get to know me better and to share my love with others. Always remember that my resurrection is the proof of my victory over death and sin, and that this victory is yours too.

# 27 October

"The Lord God made to grow out of the ground every kind of tree that is pleasant to the sight and good for food, the tree of life in the midst of the garden, and the tree of the knowledge of good and evil." (Genesis 2:9)

I invite you to reflect on the beauty and complexity of God's creation. Every tree, every flower, every creature carries within it a spark of divine providence. Let yourself be inspired by the natural world around you, and appreciate the beauty of God's creation. May this respect and love for nature inspire you to care for our planet, our common home.

# 28 October

"Hear, O Israel: the Lord our God is the only Lord."
(Deuteronomy 6:4)

Let me remind you that the Father is the only true God. He is
the creator of the universe, the author of all good things. His
faithfulness never fails. His love for you is without end. May
you turn to him in your daily life, loving him with all your
heart, with all your soul and with all your strength. May this
devotion give you the strength to overcome life's challenges
and remain firm in your faith.

# 29th October

"Love your enemies, do good to those who hate you, bless
those who curse you, pray for those who mistreat you." (Luke
6:27-28)

I invite you to go beyond divisions and conflicts. It's easy to
love those who love us, but the real challenge is to love those
who have hurt us. It is by reaching out to those who have hurt
us that we can truly live the love of Christ. Remember that
forgiveness is the first step towards healing.

# 30 October

"Seek first the kingdom of God and his righteousness, and all these things will be added to you." (Matthew 6:33)

I remind you that your real treasure lies in the kingdom of God. All the riches of the world cannot compare with the peace and joy of a close relationship with the Father. So put God first in your lives, and you will see that all other things will be given to you in addition. Live in God's love, and you will live in abundance.

# 31 October

"And whatever you ask in prayer, if you believe, you will receive." (Matthew 21:22)

I would remind you that prayer is a powerful communication with God. When you pray with faith, sincerely believing that God is able to answer your prayers, miracles can happen. Trust in God's promise, even in difficult times, and never forget that faith can move mountains. Whether in solitude or in a crowd, sincere prayer will always be heard. God sees into the depths of our hearts and accepts our prayers with infinite love.

# 1 November

"For where two or three are gathered together in my name, there am I in the midst of them." (Matthew 18:20)

I assure you that I am always present, especially when you gather in my name. Don't forget that I'm with you in your moments of prayer, praise, sharing and love. Your shared faith creates a powerful bond that brings me closer to you. May your faith grow and flourish in fellowship. And know that whenever you seek to know and follow me, I am there, ready to guide and support you on your journey.

# 2 November

Every day is a precious gift, an opportunity to love and serve. In the rush and chaos, find moments of peace and tranquillity. When doubt assails you, remember that you can find wisdom in silence, far from the noise and bustle. In your work, do everything with love and devotion, honouring the divine in yourself and others. Your every action has an impact, being part of a greater divine plan. Every act of love and kindness you do, no matter how small, has an eternal resonance in the universe.

# 3 November

Everyday life is a mosaic of sacred moments, little graces that often go unnoticed. You are never alone, even in the darkest moments. When you feel the weight of the world on your shoulders, know that I'm here to support you, to help you carry your burdens. Find comfort in the warmth of a shared smile, in the tenderness of a loving gesture. Every moment of joy and sorrow is imbued with my love for you. Your trials and triumphs, however great or small, have inestimable meaning and value in the grand scheme of life.

# 4 November

Together, let's observe nature, an open book that teaches us. As the seasons change, each creature plays its part in the harmony of life. See how each animal, each plant, each element has its place and its importance. Like them, you are part of a magnificent whole. Cherish this connection you have with all creation and be aware of your actions and their impact on the world around you.

# 5 November

Patience is a virtue that is cultivated with time and experience. In a world that demands ever greater speed and efficiency, don't forget the power of patience. With patience, you can learn to accept the natural rhythm of things, to understand that everything has its time. With patience, you can face challenges, overcome obstacles and achieve your goals. Like a gardener who waits for the seeds he has planted to grow, have the patience to see things unfold at their own pace.

# 6 November

Change is an inevitable part of life. Change can sometimes be frightening, but know that every change brings with it new opportunities. Instead of resisting change, embrace it. See every change as a chance to learn, grow and adapt. Remember that even the most beautiful flowers must first grow through the mud. Change is an opportunity to redefine yourself, reinvent yourself and discover new facets of yourself. So when you feel the wind of change blowing, don't build a wall to block it, instead build a mill to take advantage of it.

# 7 November

Generosity is a quality that enriches not only those who receive it, but also those who give it. A generous heart does not give with the expectation of receiving in return, but because it finds joy in the act of giving. Generosity can take many forms, whether it's giving your time, your skills or your resources. Remember that every act of generosity, no matter how small, has the potential to make a big difference in someone's life. Every smile shared, every kind word spoken, every gesture of help is a reflection of the generosity of your heart. Never underestimate the power of your generosity.

# 8 November

Respect is a fundamental value that must be integrated into all aspects of our daily lives. It means not only treating others with dignity, but also respecting their opinions, feelings and rights. Respect also means accepting differences and recognising the inherent worth of each individual. When you practise respect, you create an environment where everyone can feel valued and appreciated. Remember that respect starts with yourself: respect your own limits, feelings, efforts and time.

# 9 November

Forgiveness can sometimes be difficult to give, especially when the pain is deep. However, forgiveness is not a sign of weakness, but a sign of strength. It is a decision to let go of anger, resentment and the desire for revenge. Forgiveness does not mean that you forget or excuse the wrong that has been done. It means that you choose peace over conflict, love over hate. Forgiveness frees you from the chains of anger and opens the way to healing and peace. Forgiveness is a gift you give yourself.

# 10 November

Gratitude is a powerful thing. It has the ability to transform your perspective and fill you with joy and appreciation for the things you have. Even in the most difficult of times, there's always something to be grateful for. Maybe it's the warmth of the sun on your face, the smile of a loved one, or just being alive. Expressing gratitude can help you focus on the positive aspects of your life, rather than the negative. Make gratitude a daily practice and watch how it changes your life.

# 11 November

Courage is not the absence of fear, but the willingness to face fear and carry on despite it. We all need courage in different facets of our lives, whether it's facing a challenge, making a difficult decision or simply facing a new day. Remember, courage doesn't mean that you don't feel fear, but that you don't let that fear control or hold you back. You have courage within you. Believe in yourself and your ability to overcome the challenges you face.

# 12 November

Generosity is a gift that you give to yourself as well as to others. It's not just about giving material goods, but also about giving your time, attention and love. Giving to others gives us a deep sense of joy and satisfaction, and creates stronger bonds with those around us. Try to find ways to be generous every day. You may be surprised at how much it can enrich your life. Always remember that every act of generosity, no matter how small, can make a big difference in someone's life. Your generosity can inspire others to be generous too.

## 13 November

Patience is an essential virtue for navigating through life. Just as a gardener must wait for his seeds to germinate and grow, we must also learn to wait for the good things in life. It can be frustrating not to see immediate results, but remember that growth takes time. Do your best, be patient, and trust the process. Things will fall into place at the right time. Be patient with yourself and with others. Remember that everyone moves at their own pace and it's important to respect that. Patience can be a source of peace and serenity in an often hectic world.

## 14 November

Loneliness is a feeling that all of us experience from time to time. It is in these moments of solitude that we are invited to turn inward, to reflect on our lives and what we really want. It's an opportunity to understand and appreciate yourself. It's important to remember that even in these moments, you're never really alone. Every day, look for quiet moments to reconnect with yourself and enjoy your own company. Cherish these moments of solitude as moments of self-reflection and personal growth.

## 15 November

Friendship is one of life's greatest gifts. It's a relationship based on mutual love, respect and understanding. Friends are the people who support you through good times and bad, who help you grow and develop. They are a source of joy, comfort and support. Cherish your friends and do all you can to nurture these precious relationships. Take the time to connect with them, share your thoughts and feelings, and listen to what they have to say. Remember that friendship isn't about quantity, it's about quality. A true friend is a blessing, and true love is a treasure to be treasured.

## 16 November

Seek comfort in shared love, in the gentleness of two hearts coming together. The couple is a reflection of my will, a place to grow, to forgive, to love unconditionally. In the days of joy as in the days of storm, remember that love is patient, love is understanding. Allow your love to become a light, a source of inspiration for others. Have faith in the strength of your union and your love, for it is through this that you can truly evolve. Make the sweetness of your time together, the strength of your love, your sanctuary, your place of refuge and peace.

# 17 November

On this day, let's remember the importance of our health, the most precious treasure we have ever been given. It is the harmony of mind, body and soul. Take care of your health, it's the vehicle for your mission on earth. With every breath, every movement, give thanks for this priceless gift. Take a moment each day to recognise the beauty of your body and mind. Your health is your strength, your vital energy. Don't neglect it, but nurture it with love and gratitude. Celebrate the life within you, the marvellous mechanism that sustains you, and devote yourself to preserving and nurturing it.

# 18 November

In this race for professional success, remember that the real victory lies not in promotion, pay rise or recognition, but in the love you put into your work. The joy you find in what you do is invaluable. By finding satisfaction in your work, you'll find meaning and value in what you do, and that's worth more than any salary or job title. Know that every task accomplished with passion and dedication is a victory in itself. Don't let superficial definitions of success lead you astray from your authentic path.

# 19 November

In this modern age, where landmarks sometimes seem to be lost, I encourage you to look for what is constant and true. Find calm in the midst of chaos, love in the midst of indifference, truth in the midst of fake news. Stay anchored in what really matters to you, in what gives meaning to your life, even when the world around you seems to be losing its meaning. It's in these moments of doubt that we find our true strength and direction. Each of us has an inner beacon that can guide us through the storms of life, so trust that beacon and allow it to guide you towards peace and serenity.

# 20 November

In an increasingly connected world, we mustn't forget the importance of genuine human relationships. Whether with friends, family or even strangers, every interaction we have is a chance to touch someone else's life and leave a positive mark. Let's show compassion, empathy and kindness to others. And let's not forget that even the smallest acts of kindness can make a big difference to someone's life. Let's cherish these moments of genuine human connection, because they are the pillars of our humanity. What's more, let's remember that our relationships with others can be a source of joy and fulfilment. So let's make every day an opportunity to improve our relationships with those around us, to create a more caring and loving world.

# 21 November

The journey towards independence can be difficult and full of pitfalls. There may be times when you feel lost, overwhelmed and exhausted. But don't forget that these moments are part of the process of learning and growing. Every trial you go through makes you stronger and more resilient. Learn to trust yourself, to support yourself and to believe in your ability to overcome the obstacles that stand in your way. You are capable of more than you think. Even in moments of doubt, remember that you have the strength and courage within you to keep going. And remember that every step you take towards autonomy brings you closer to your highest potential. So, even though the path may be difficult, keep moving forward with determination, because every step counts in your journey towards autonomy.

# 22 November

In a society that values productivity and speed, we can sometimes forget the importance of taking the time to stop, breathe and simply be. We mustn't let the pressure of time deprive us of moments of tranquillity and serenity. Whether through meditation, reading or simply taking the time to enjoy a cup of tea, let's find ways to slow down and reconnect with ourselves. These moments of calm are essential for our mental and emotional well-being, and they help us keep a balanced perspective in our hectic daily lives.

# 23 November

We live in an age of constant and often rapid change. These changes can sometimes be a source of stress and anxiety. But remember that change can also be an opportunity for growth and renewal. Whether it's a change of job, home or even mindset, every change is a chance to start a new chapter in your life. Don't be afraid of change, but embrace it with an open and positive attitude. And remember, although change can be uncomfortable, it is often the prelude to beautiful transformations.

# 24 November

Every day we make decisions that shape our lives. Some are small, others have a bigger impact. It's essential to remember that every choice we make matters. The act of deciding is not just an intellectual exercise, but an act of responsibility towards ourselves. So, even if we make mistakes, every choice is an opportunity for growth and learning. Let's not fear mistakes, but see them as a chance to evolve and progress.

## 25 November

Human relationships are at the heart of our existence. It is important to cultivate and maintain healthy, positive relationships with others. However, in our day-to-day interactions, we can sometimes encounter conflicts and misunderstandings. When this happens, it's crucial to communicate openly and honestly, to listen to each other and to respect each other's points of view. Let's remember that everyone we meet has their own story and their own experiences, and that it's essential to show empathy and understanding in our relationships.

## 26 November

Remember, my children, forgiveness is one of the keys to opening the gates of the kingdom of heaven. It can be difficult to free your heart from the pain caused by others, but forgiveness is a gift you give to yourself. When you forgive, you lay down the heavy burden of bitterness and allow yourself freedom and peace. I'm with you in this process. Even if the past cannot be changed, you have the choice of how you react to your experiences. When you forgive, you open up the possibility of growing and learning valuable lessons. It is through forgiveness that you will find the serenity and love to move forward.

## 27 November

Don't let yourself be distracted by comparisons with others. Your value is not measured by the successes of others, because you all have a unique path to travel. You are each precious in my eyes, and you all have unique talents that are a blessing to the world. Focus on your own growth and development, celebrate every little victory you achieve along the way. Be proud of yourself, of who you are, because each of you is a wonderful creation of God. Remember that your journey is unique and that every step you take is part of the work of art that God has designed for you. I'm with you every step of the way.

## 28 November

In your moments of solitude, remember that you are never really alone. I'm always with you, with every breath, every heartbeat. It's in those moments of silence that you can really hear my voice and feel my presence. Look for me in solitude and you will find me, not as a distant presence, but as a faithful friend at your side, ready to share your sorrows and joys. Solitude can be a space to draw close to me, to rest in me and to discover me in the depths of your soul.

## 29 November

Friendship is a precious gift, a reflection of my love for you. Cherish your friends, for they are fellow travellers who share life's joys and sorrows with you. Show them love, kindness and understanding, for it is in giving that we receive. Just as I have loved you, love your friends unconditionally, without expecting anything in return. It's in authentic friendship that you discover the depth of my love for you, a love that doesn't judge, that doesn't play favourites, but that embraces each of you as you are.

## 30 November

I know that some of you are feeling overwhelmed by the daily challenges. Know that I am with you. I am your support, your strength and your refuge. Even in the midst of storms, keep the faith. Remain strong and courageous, for I am with you. Don't let uncertainty make you doubt your worth or your purpose. You are precious to me, and I want you to fulfil your potential. Don't forget that you have the strength within you to overcome any obstacle. Trust in my unfailing love to guide you through the difficult times.

# 1 December

In your quest for work-life balance, remember that I am the master of time. You can turn to me for wisdom and guidance. Trust me with your concerns and worries, and I'll give you the peace you seek. I am aware of your needs and I want to give you the rest you deserve. Know that I am with you through every decision, every task and every moment of your life. Never forget that my love for you transcends all the pressures and challenges you may face.

# 2 December

I see every effort you make to lead a just and honest life. Don't be discouraged if the results of your efforts are not immediate. Every step you take towards goodness, however small, has value in my eyes. The importance lies in consistency and perseverance. So don't tire of doing good. Every act of kindness, every word of love, every gesture of support - I see them all and I promise you that they will bear fruit in due course. Rest assured that your work will not be in vain, because the good you do reflects the light of my love. Keep moving forward, step by step, day by day. Your resilience and determination will lead you to the fulfilment of your dreams and aspirations.

# 3 December

You're precious to me, and I'm always there for you, even in the darkest of times. I know that you are going through difficult times, but don't forget that I am your refuge and your strength. Your trials may be great, but my love for you is even greater. Do not lose hope, for I have promised never to leave you or forsake you. I am with you, now and always, and I will bring you the peace and comfort you need. I'm by your side, supporting every step you take, wiping away every tear you shed. Remember that the darkness of the night does not prevent the dawn from breaking. Keep your faith in me, and together we'll get through this.

# 4 December

I understand when you feel the weight of the world on your shoulders. Sometimes you feel so overwhelmed by responsibilities and expectations that you don't know where to start. But remember, I'm with you every step of the way. Don't be discouraged, don't be afraid. I'm here to support and guide you. Go forward with confidence and courage, knowing that I'm here to help you. Find comfort in the fact that I'm always with you, ready to lighten your load when you're tired and overwhelmed. Let me be your strength and support in times of doubt and uncertainty.

## 5 December

Each of you is unique and precious to me. I created you with care and love, and I love you more than you could ever imagine. I understand your worries and doubts, your fears and anxieties. But I invite you to entrust all these concerns to me, to trust me. Because I promise to always be there for you, to help and guide you. I will never leave you alone, even in the darkest moments. Take the time to talk to me, to share your thoughts and feelings with me. I'm always there to listen to you, to offer you my love and consolation. Together, we'll overcome every obstacle.

## 6 December

I see the struggle many of you endure to find your place in this world, trying to understand your purpose and your role. Know that you are here for a reason, every life has a precious and unique purpose. Look within, listen to the quiet voice of your heart. That's where you'll find the answers you're looking for. Don't be discouraged if the path is difficult and uncertain, for I am at your side, guiding your steps. Trust in the process of life, and know that every experience, however difficult, shapes you and helps you to become the person you are destined to be.

# 7 December

I am aware of the extent of the pain that some of you are enduring. The wounds of the heart and spirit are often more painful and deeper than those of the body. I want you to know that I am with you in your suffering. I invite you to confide your pain in me, to share your burden with me. Don't isolate yourself in your suffering, because I'm here to support you and help you heal. There is always hope, even in the darkest moments. Let me bring you the peace and comfort you need.

# 8 December

I feel the despair of those who feel lost, disconnected and directionless. Don't forget that even in the darkest moments, I'm here. Even if you can't see me, I'm with you. Even if you can't hear me, I'm talking to you. Look for me in the calm and silence. Trust me to guide you, to help you find your way back. Let me be your beacon in the night, leading you to safety and peace. Your value lies not in your ability to navigate perfectly, but in your courage to keep going even when the path is difficult. Embrace uncertainty with faith, knowing that I am your constant guide.

# 9 December

I'm with those who face challenges and trials that seem insurmountable. Know that nothing is impossible with me by your side. Together, we can overcome any obstacle, solve any problem and get over any hurdle. Don't give up hope. Stay strong, stay resolute, stay faithful. With me by your side, you have everything you need to triumph. Know that every challenge you face is an opportunity for you to grow and learn. Each trial is a moment for you to learn to trust, to persevere and to have hope. So even in the moments of struggle, you can find a hidden blessing.

# 10 December

I can see the sorrow in the hearts of some of you, and I invite you to let go and open yourselves to the joy that is always at hand. Joy is not a destination, but a path. It's a choice you make every day, every moment. Even in the darkest moments, joy can be found by recognising the blessings that surround you. So choose joy. Choose to see the good, the beautiful, the sacred in every moment. Choose to celebrate the life you have been given, and know that I rejoice with you.

# 11 December

I am love incarnate and I am present in each one of you. Love is your true nature, your divine essence. Love is the force that binds you all together. It is stronger than hate, more powerful than fear. When you open yourself to love, you open yourself to me. So love with all your heart, all your mind, all your soul. Love your neighbour as yourself. Know that in every act of love, however small, I am there. And every time you choose love, you choose to let my light shine in the world.

# 12 December

Charity is a reflection of my love for you, a gesture of love that you make to your neighbour. It's a way in which you can share my light and goodness with the world. Every act of generosity, big or small, has the power to touch lives, to bring comfort, to bring hope. So share selflessly, give without expectation of return, and know that every act of charity is an echo of my compassion and mercy. For in truth, what you do for the least of my brothers and sisters, you do for me.

# 13 December

I see the hatred that can creep into your hearts, and I invite you to choose love instead. Hate is only fear in disguise, and it only leads to suffering and division. Every time you choose to hate, you distance yourself from me. But know this, it is never too late to choose love. Even in moments of anger and resentment, love is always at hand. So let go of the hatred. Forgive those who have hurt you. Choose love, and know that I'm with you every step of the way.

# 14 December

True joy does not depend on external circumstances, but comes from within, from the deep knowledge of my unconditional love for you. Sometimes the challenges and difficulties of life can obscure that joy, but remember, even in the midst of storms, my peace and joy are always available to you. So seek that inner joy, that peace of mind that comes from knowing that you are loved and cherished by me. Let this joy infuse every aspect of your life, your relationships, your work, your leisure. May the joy of the Lord be your strength.

# 15 December

Love is the greatest of all virtues. It is the very essence of who I am. And I call on you to love as I have loved you. To love unconditionally, to love without prejudice, to love even those who have hurt you. Know that love has the power to heal wounds, to bridge divisions and to transform the world. But above all, don't forget to love yourself, because you are a reflection of my glory and my love. May this love that I have shown you guide you in all your actions and all your relationships.

# 16 December

Charity is not only an act of giving, but also an act of love and compassion towards others. I invite you to practise charity in your daily lives. Don't underestimate the power of small acts of kindness, because every act of charity has the potential to profoundly touch the life of another person. When practising charity, remember that it is in giving that we receive. So give generously and sincerely, without expecting anything in return, and you will find great satisfaction and deep joy in serving others.

## 17 December

Hatred is a negative emotion that can poison your soul and distance you from my love. I invite you to reject hatred and embrace love. Remember that each of you is created in my image and that you are all my beloved children. Even in the face of injustice, choose to respond with love and compassion. Seek to understand others, to forgive their faults and to love unconditionally, as I have loved you. Then you will live in the light of my love and help to create a world of peace and harmony.

## 18 December

My creativity, which shaped the heavens and the earth, also lives in you. Every idea, every dream, every invention is an echo of My own creativity. Use this ability to build, to create, to bring beauty and joy to this world. Let your creativity be a reflection of My love and My light. Let your imagination lead you towards new perspectives, open new doors and illuminate less travelled paths. In your quest to create, remember that every thought and every action contributes to a greater symphony of life. Keep dreaming, inventing and pushing yourself. Your creativity is a true gift, an extension of My own essence. Never forget how precious you are in this vast web of creation.

# 19 December

Nature is a precious gift that I have created for you. The mountains, the rivers, the forests, every part of the earth is a manifestation of My creativity and My love. Take care of this gift, cherish it, protect it. By preserving nature, you honour My creation. Don't forget that every blade of grass, every leaf that falls, every animal that roams the earth is part of this great plan of love and life. Harmony with nature is harmony with Myself. Appreciate the splendour of every sunrise and sunset, the tranquillity of every lake, the majesty of every mountain. Your respect and love for nature are a reflection of your love for Me.

# 20 December

I created you with an inquisitive mind, always ready to learn, explore and understand. This quest for knowledge is a reflection of my love for discovery and truth. Keep searching, keep questioning, keep learning. Every piece of knowledge you acquire brings you closer to me and helps you to better understand the world I have created. Never be discouraged by the unknown or by uncertainty, because it's in these moments that true growth takes place. Keep in mind that knowledge is not just an end in itself, but a means of serving others and making a difference in the world.

# 21 December

I would like you to find in me the serenity that can sometimes elude you in the tumult of life. Take a moment each day to seek that tranquillity in your heart. Let me bring you the calm and peace you need to face life's challenges. Serenity is not the absence of conflict or difficulty, but the ability to remain calm and centred in the midst of life's storms. Know that I am always with you, whether you are on the mountain top or in the darkest valley. Seek serenity in me, and you will find the strength and tranquillity you need to navigate life's journey.

# 22 December

Freedom, my beloved, is a precious gift that I have entrusted to you. It allows you to choose the good and to distance yourselves from evil. It gives you the opportunity to grow, to love and to forgive. I invite you to use this freedom to live in accordance with my will, to love others as I love you. But don't forget that true freedom is not to do whatever you want, but to do what is right, even if it's difficult. Cherish this freedom, use it wisely and it will lead you to a rich and fulfilling life.

## 23 December

Integrity is a virtue that I cherish, because it reflects the truth of who you are. When you live with integrity, you are true to yourself, to your values, and you are a reflection of my love and truth in the world. Integrity requires courage, because it often forces you to swim against the tide, to resist the temptation to take the easy way out. But know that I am always by your side, supporting and guiding your steps along the path of integrity. When you show integrity, you shine like a light in the world, a reflection of my love and truth.

## 24 December

Humility is a virtue that I greatly value. Humility doesn't mean devaluing yourself or ignoring your talents and abilities. Rather, it means recognising that everything you have and everything you are comes from me. It means understanding that I love you unconditionally and that your value does not depend on your successes or failures. Humility keeps you open to my love and grace, and helps you to serve others with compassion and generosity. When you live with humility, you are a reflection of my love in the world.

# 25 December

On this special day, the day of my birth, I am with you. I hear your prayers, I feel your sorrows and joys, and I am with you every moment.

This is a day of rejoicing, a day to commemorate the unconditional love I have brought into the world. I hope that this love will resonate in your hearts and that it will manifest itself in your actions towards others.

I invite you to celebrate not only my birth, but also the promise of renewal that it brings. Like the bright star that guided the Magi to the stable, let your faith guide you to the light in the darkness.

On this day, I remind you that every act of kindness, every word of love and every gesture of compassion is a reflection of the Christmas spirit. It is in me that you find the strength to overcome challenges and the ability to bring comfort to those in need.

As you rejoice and show kindness to others, remember that I was born to show you the way of love and salvation. I have walked among you, shared your joys and sorrows, and demonstrated the incredible power of love.

On this day, may your hearts rejoice in the wonderful promise of love, hope and joy that my birth brings to everyone. May peace be with you, now and always. Amen.

# **26 December**

This day after my birth, I am among you, I see your actions and feel your emotions. I bring you the promise of love, compassion and kindness that my presence in this world signifies.

Today, I invite you to rejoice in the spirit of sharing and caring that the festive season embodies. I ask you to keep this spirit alive, not just during this season, but throughout the year.

Remember that I am always with you, in every moment of joy, sorrow, success and challenge. Each of you has the capacity to reflect my goodness and love towards others, and every act of kindness counts.

I ask you to be patient and understanding with those around you, and to remember that each person is a reflection of my love. You can make a difference in the lives of others through your actions and words, and I am with you every step of the way.

As you go about your day, remember that you are loved, that you are precious and that you have the power to spread love and goodness in the world. In me you find the strength to face challenges and the ability to bring comfort to those in need. Remain in my love. Amen.

# 27 December

On this day, I see the lights of your souls blossoming, like the first rays of sunlight after a long night. You are awakening to a new day, full of opportunities and possibilities.

I invite you to take a moment to express your gratitude for all the blessings you have received, no matter how small. Every blessing is a gift from me, and I hope you find joy and comfort in every glimmer of goodness and grace.

As you go about your day, remember to look for opportunities to show kindness and love to those around you. Every act of kindness, every kind word, has the power to bring a glimmer of hope and joy into the world.

Remember that I'm always with you, ready to support and guide you on your journey. May my presence be your comfort and strength, and may my love for you always be a source of peace and joy.

When in doubt, turn to me. When you need comfort, look for me. I'm here, ready to welcome you with love and compassion. In every moment, I'm there by your side, guiding you with love and compassion. Stay in my love. Amen.

## 28 December

I want you to know that my love for you is infinite and unwavering. No matter what trials you go through, I am at your side to help you overcome them. I hear your prayers and your deepest desires. Today, I encourage you to surrender yourself completely to me, to have faith in my presence and in my power to transform.

Take a moment to immerse yourself in my peace and love. Know that every difficulty you encounter is an opportunity to grow and draw closer to me. Let me carry your burdens, let me relieve you of your worries. Always remember my unconditional love for you. Continue to seek my face, to draw near to me, and I will fill you with my grace and my peace. Amen.

## 29 December

Today I'm asking you to be patient. It's normal to have moments of uncertainty and questioning, but remember that I'm with you every step of the way. Let me be your anchor in the storms of life. Find comfort in me and know that my will for you is perfect.

Don't forget that my time is not yours. Even if things don't go the way you want, trust me. I'm working in you and through you, even if you can't see it. Let me guide you through the mountains and valleys of life. Be patient, be strong, be courageous. Always remember that I am your refuge and your strength, an ever-present help in trouble. Amen.

# 30th December

Dear children, I'm here in the midst of your daily turmoil. I see your struggles and I know the depths of your hearts. Today, I invite you to let go of your fear and embrace trust. Know that you are not alone, that you are loved and precious in my eyes.

I am the guardian of your soul and I hold your every breath in my hand. So, when trials come your way, remember this truth. Fear is not from me. Courage, hope and love come from me. In me you will find peace and comfort. In me you will find the true meaning of your existence.

# 31 December

On this last day of the year, I invite you to reflect. Think back on all the moments you've experienced this year, the joys, the sorrows, the challenges and the victories. It's through these experiences that you grow and become closer to me. Don't be afraid to look back, because every moment is precious to me.

Let past mistakes teach you and help you grow, but don't let them define you. You are much more than your mistakes. You are my beloved children, created in my image. As the New Year dawns, I invite you to welcome change, to open your hearts to new possibilities, and to walk with faith and courage along the path I have prepared for you.

Made in the USA
Las Vegas, NV
07 February 2024

85472105R00105